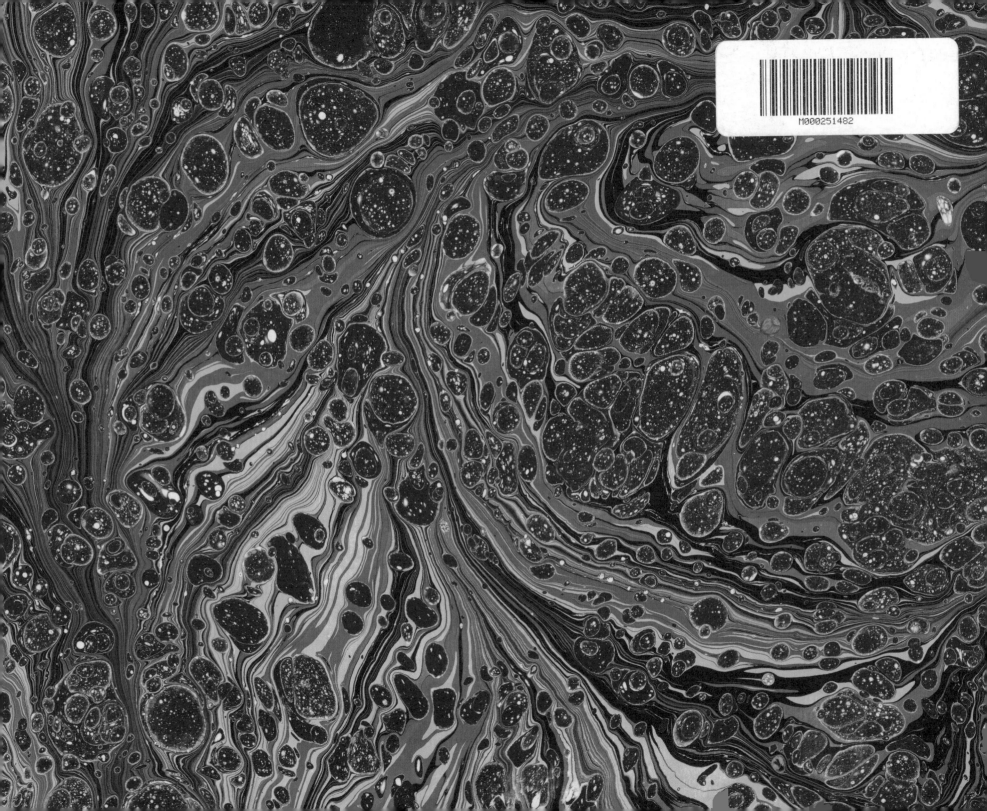

Mercedes-Benz 770K

Hitler arrives in Berlin Grosser license plate 1A-103708 at a Hitler Youth/HJ rally at Nürnberg before the war. Chauffeur Erich Kempka is driving, and Deputy Führer Rudolf Hess sits at left rear. The *Führerstandarte/Leader Standard* is in place at left. The car is an Experimental W 24 type. (Hermann Göring Albums, Library of Congress, Wash., DC.)

Hitler's Chariots

Vol 2

Mercedes-Benz 770K

Grosser Parade Car

Blaine Taylor

Schiffer Military History
Atglen, PA

Book Design by Ian Robertson and Stephanie Daugherty.

Printed in China.
ISBN: 978-0-7643-3521-1

We are interested in hearing from authors with book ideas on related topics.

Published by Schiffer Publishing Ltd.
4880 Lower Valley Road
Atglen, PA 19310
Phone: (610) 593-1777
FAX: (610) 593-2002
E-mail: Info@schifferbooks.com.
Visit our web site at: www.schifferbooks.com
Please write for a free catalog.
This book may be purchased from the publisher.
Please include $5.00 postage.
Try your bookstore first.

In Europe, Schiffer books are distributed by:
Bushwood Books
6 Marksbury Avenue
Kew Gardens
Surrey TW9 4JF, England
Phone: 44 (0) 20 8392-8585
FAX: 44 (0) 20 8392-9876
E-mail: Info@bushwoodbooks.co.uk.
Visit our website at: www.bushwoodbooks.co.uk

Contents

Introduction 8

Chapter 1:   Porsche, Daimler, and the Creation of the Supercharger.................................... 9
Chapter 2:   The "Chauffeureska" - Hitler's Driver/Bodyguards and the *Kampfzeit* 57
Chapter 3:   The 770K Grosser Model 79
Chapter 4:   Hitler's Chariots in Use 107
Chapter 5:   Motorcades 150
Chapter 6:   The Survivors — 1945 and Afterward 198

Appendix A: Four Historic—But Little Known!—Auto Accidents 213
Appendix B: Color Gallery 217
              Bibliography 239

Dedication

To the dearly departed:

Maryland State Sen. Patrick T. Welsh (D, 7th, MD), Taylor campaign manager Michael F. Marino, campaign worker Dona Amici, noted Civil War reenactor and Napoleonic Wars writer Brian C. Pohanka, and Towson Penthouse rental agent Maxine Van Wright. All are greatly missed by the author.

Acknowledgments

Photographer Stan Piet of the Glenn L. Martin Aviation Museum, Martin State Airport, Middle River, MD; Maria Feifel of DaimlerChrysler AG Konzernarchiv, Stüttgart-Untertürkheim, Germany; Roger Wychgram of Aberdeen, MD;; and P. James Kurapka, Gate City, VA.

The Führer's 770K Grosser serves as a backdrop to this photo of Reich Master of the Hunt and German Forests Hermann Göring (left) and Hitler (right) at the former's *Karinhall* estate outside Berlin on July 5, 1935. Note that the *Führerstandarte/Leader Standard* is affixed on the right front of the vehicle. Reportedly, Göring's humane game laws are still on the books in Germany to this day. (HGA, LC, Wash., DC.)

Sieg Heil! Hail Victory! Hitler and his entourage drive in Berlin license plate IA-148764 for his mammoth 50th birthday parade of April 20, 1939. The famed *Siegestor/Victory Column* can be seen in the far distance, where American Democratic Party Presidential candidate U.S. Sen. Barack Obama spoke in 2008. (HHA, USNA, College Park, MD)

Introduction:
"A city block long"

Few Germans owned automobiles until the *Volkswagen/People's Car* revolution of post-1949, yet Hitler—the rising politician—owned an entire fleet of *Grosser/Grand*, or *Greater* Mercedes.

Even today, Daimler-Benz and Mercedes-Benz advertise its cars as, "The finest automobiles in the world." Hitler appeared all over Germany in his long, shiny limousines, either riding on a lonely country lane or standing upright, taking the salute of his men at innumerable marches-past.

In the following pages we shall see Hitler and these amazing cars in both simple, roadside scenes, as well as in all the panoply of the lost, shattered power of the long fallen Nazi Third Reich.

Blaine Taylor
Berkshires at Town Center
Towson, MD/USA
November 1, 2009

Hitler's car—or cars, as there were a great many in existence by the time of the 1945 *Zusammenbruch*/collapse—were for many Germans a visible, tangible proof of their *Führer's* greatness and importance. Chauffeur SS Julius Schreck drives. (HHA, USNA, College Park, MD.)

8

Porsche, Daimler, and the Creation of the Supercharger

Hitler's Cars: The 770K Grossers
Only 117 770K *Grosser/Grand* Mercedes were ever built, so far as is now known.

The unique and elite 1938 770K model was the "company flagship," and had a top speed of 100 mph. Daimler introduced the 7.7-liter Grosser in 1930, when only a very few were at first built—for movie stars and foreign rulers, mainly. Authors Boesin and Grad refer to it as a "monster." All of the "Führer cars" boasted seven passenger seats and extra side windows.

There were two generations of Grosser Mercedes: the WO 7, manufactured during 1930-38; and the W 150, built during 1938-43, all with the now famous chromium-plated exhaust pipes coming out of the right side of the engines. Indeed, according to noted Swedish car expert and author Jan Melin, these shiny pipes were "The hallmark of the big Mercedes-Benz cars during the 1930s."

Mercedes titan Jakob Werlin ordered a special 770K Grosser Mercedes Cabriolet D with four doors and seven seats to be made as a presentation gift for Hitler's 50th birthday on April 20, 1939, with 18mm-thick armor plating, 40mm-thick bullet proof windows, and explosion-proof, 20-chamber cellular tires, as well as side-mounted spare tires housed in the twin wings enclosed compartments.

Sausages and Beer with the Nazi *Führer*
During one of their early automotive design meetings, German Chancellor Adolf Hitler asked the famed car designer Dr. Ferdinand Porsche (1875-1951), "I've arranged for sausages and beer. OK?" It was, and the two men proceeded to make automotive and military vehicular history together.

According to Dr. Ferry Porsche (the Elder's son), writing in his own 1976 memoirs, *We at Porsche,* "At the 1925 Solitude road race...outside Stüttgart...Hitler—who was a close friend of Dr. Richard Voelter, the advertising director of the Daimler Company—happened to be there as a spectator, along with some of his associates...Voelter introduced my father to the future Chancellor." Even stranger, perhaps, the latter never forgot this encounter, which was to have some far-reaching consequences in later years.

Although the swastika disappeared in 1945, the world-renowned three-pointed Mercedes-Benz encircled star dominated the car world both before and since, as now. (Daimler Museum, Stüttgart, Germany.)

Their second meeting—which occurred in 1934 after Hitler had taken office as Chancellor—was set up by their mutual friend and car associate, Werlin.

Dr. Porsche—initially trained as a plumber—was born on September 8, 1875, in Maffersdorf, in Bohemia. Through hard work and diligent study Porsche became a self-taught engineer, working for the Löhner Automobile Factory in Austria's Imperial capital, Vienna, where, in 1900, he built an electric car with a rotary motor.

Six years later, he joined the Austro-Daimler Company, and a decade after that was named its General Director. The firm built internal combustion engines that garnered both the firm and its talented engineer international acclaim.

Porsche became world famous at the 1900 Paris Universal Exposition, and built an electric car with both four-wheel-drive and brakes that was powered by two-ton batteries (!) He abandoned these because, "The weight was too great and the range too short," leading him to then combine gas with electric power. "The engine drove a generator that charged the batteries that ran the car." The gearbox was also eliminated.

During 1901-06 Dr. Porsche worked for the Löhner firm, asserting that, "My first meal is at midnight." Indeed, while viewing the Follies Bergere at Paris, he stated that the dancing girls' legs reminded him of carburetors!

During the Great War of 1914-18, Dr. Porsche built 80-ton gun carriages for the Imperial Austrian Army that were really large tractors in today's terms, working with 20-year-old Army officer Alfred Neubauer, later both a famous race car driver and a Mercedes racing team manager.

After the defeated Central Powers lost the First World War, Dr. Porsche found himself in 1923 at the Daimler Motor Company plant at Stüttgart, Germany. Ironically, Dr. Porsche was fated to succeed the founder's son, Paul Daimler, twice as Technical Director: first in 1906 at the Austro-Daimler Works, and then again in 1923 at the Daimler plant at Untertürkheim, Germany. Hans Nibel helped him as joint engineer.

Enter the Straight-8 Kompressors

Noted car author Roger Bell states in *Great Marques: Mercedes-Benz*, "One of his first tasks was to complete the two-liter, straight-eight, supercharged racing car—started by Paul Daimler—to replace the 1.5- and two-liter, four-cylinder, full-blown cars that scored a number of successes in the 1920s."

Fully embracing both the spirit and practicality of the elephantine *Kompressor/Compressor* superchargers, Dr. Porsche went on to build all of the great sporting "S" cars of the Twenties and Thirties, starting in 1927 with the S (Sports), SS (Super Sport), SSKurz (Super Sport Short), and SSKLong.

According to *Classic Mercedes-Benz*, "Mercedes led the field...There was nothing to touch them." During 1928 alone, the S won 53 times, breaking 17 world records in the process.

The irascible Dr. Porsche the Elder had a notoriously short temper. Once, Dr. Wilhelm Kissel left eight Stüttgart models out in the open one freezing night, and the next morning challenged an enraged Dr. Porsche to start any of them. He couldn't. Thus, he resigned from Mercedes-Benz on December 31, 1928, to found his own design firm, leaving Hans Nibel in charge as sole engineer.

Dr. Ferdinand Porsche the Elder died at Stüttgart on January 30, 1951, ironically the 17th anniversary of Hitler's appointment as German Reich Chancellor in 1933.

The Advent of Paul Daimler

Automotive developments during 1885-1919 were: inventors Carl Benz and Gottlieb Daimler built the first true cars in 1885; Emil Jellinek and Wilhelm Maybach were jointly responsible for the manufacture of the initial Mercedes model during 1900-01, while Paul Daimler and Dr. Porsche the Elder are jointly credited with the making of the premier supercharger.

Asserted noted car authoress Beverly Rae Kimes, "The Mercedes was the first car in the world to be offered with the supercharger as standard equipment." In June 1923, Dr. Porsche left Austro-Daimler for Stüttgart to take over from Paul Daimler for the second time. Dr. Porsche was then noted as "The foremost engine man" of the day, as well as a "difficult genius and a bellwether." He inaugurated the famed K cars in 1926.

At Stüttgart, Dr, Porsche took over the efforts to build a supercharger first begun by Paul Daimler.

The Supercharger Arrives

The supercharger—or blown engine—had initially been developed by Daimler as early as 1915 (as did Benz the next year) for the fighter aircraft of the Imperial German Army Air Corps during World War I, providing them with an additional horsepower boost. Paul Daimler developed the feature for cars during 1919-21, and it was duly introduced as the Type 10/40/65 Roadster at the 1922 Berlin International Automobile and Motorcycle Show.

For Paul Daimler, the supercharger was the most important engineering achievement of his career, most of which he'd spent in the long shadow of his more famous father, Gottlieb Daimler. Although it was to prove to be an expensive "add-on," as patron Hitler asserted, "If the customer wants it, he will pay for it," as, indeed, they did.

The real drive toward the foundation of the supercharger era began in 1924 under the direction of Dr. Porsche, "The man who would exploit" it to the full, according to one source. He would develop—besides the Mannheim and Stüttgart models—the six-cylinder S, SS, and SSK series. The latter had what was known as "the elephant blower," the larger Kompressor built up to 1928.

Noted author Ken Dalleson, "When the blower's engaged, does it ever roar! The noise alone will blast the others off the road!" Authors Boesin and Grad liken the sound of a supercharger to "A rising howl." The later eight-cylinder superchargers were built *by hand*, not on an assembly line.

Added Dalleson, "the supercharger provided power, acceleration, and top-end speeds of over 100 mph, from a low snarl to an ear-shattering screech."

The Supercharger's Golden Age, 1934-39

Despite its 1921 design and 1922 formal introduction, the real era of the supercharged cars was the Golden Age of 1934-39, when they became highly visible to the entire world through the movie newsreels of the era as Hitler's chariots.

According to author Jonathan Wood's *Great Marques of Germany*, "The supercharger was not permanently engaged, but came into operation when the throttle was fully depressed, and did so via a multi-plate clutch. This meant that the blower was operating at three-four times crankshaft speed. It was to feature on selected Mercedes-Benz passenger cars until 1939, and was incorporated in all the racing cars" of the Thirties.

In part because of the 770K Grosser's close identification with Hitler and the Nazis, the superchargers have not been produced since the end of World War II in 1945, but they may *yet* reappear one day when kings, dictators, and presidents want to be chauffeured about in their like once more.

How Many Were Built?

Expert Jan Melin asserts that 117 Grosser Mercedes were manufactured in the first production generation, followed by 88 in the second, with an additional 75 of the wartime G-4 cross-country cars being built (see Volume 1 in this series).

As I stated in my 2004 work *Apex of Glory*, "The question as to how many were built was hampered, Melin believed, by the wartime Allied bombings that destroyed many relevant documents. Another difficulty in achieving an accurate count was that, many times, two or even three bodies had been used on a single chassis during the life of a car, and the numbers pertained to the chassis plates, and *not* the bodies.

"Despite this however, Melin asserted that there were few 'human errors' in his search of Daimler-Benz records." Production lists were drawn up in 1940, 1944, and later. There were two types of dates: delivery and chassis, with the latter being the actual date the car was built. The chassis and engine figures were identical.

According to the 1940 and 1944 lists, there were built at Untertürkheim the following Grossers (W07/W107): four in 1930, 42 in 1931, nine in 1932, four in 1933, 11 in 1934, 10 in 1936, 13 in 1937, and another 13 in 1938, for a total of 117. Of the W150 class, there were 13 manufactured in 1938, 44 in 1939, one in 1940, one in 1941, 10 in 1942, and 19 in 1943, for a total of 88 units.

In terms of body types, 119 Grosser Mercedes (W07/W107), 88 Grosser Mercedes (W150), and six Experimental (W24) were built at Sindelfingen.

Near Right: Dr. Ferdinand Porsche the Elder, 1875-1951. (DBM.)

Far Right: Car inventor Carl Benz, 1844-1929. (DBM.)

Hans Nibel (1880-1934) succeeded Dr. Porsche as Chief Engineer at Daimler-Benz, having begun his own career with the firm in 1908. Nibel died in 1934, the second year of the Third Reich. He developed both the SSK and the SSKL. (Mercedes-Benz Albums, Library of Congress, Wash., DC.)

Chancellor Hitler (left center) congratulates Imperial German Army Gen. Karl Litzmann (1850-1936) on the latter's 85th birthday. Looking on at second from right is Daimler-Benz official Jakob Werlin, who as a salesman sold Hitler his very first Mercedes. Notes German author Wulf Schwarzwäller in *The Unknown Hitler*, "Hitler's Münich friend—Mercedes representative Jakob Werlin—later climbed to the very top in the corporation"; indeed, as Hitler's man, both within Daimler and also overall, in charge of the German car industry. (HHA.)

Car inventor Gottleib Daimler, 1834-1900. (DBM.)

Supercharger inventor Paul Daimler, 1869-1945. (DBM.)

Mercedes model creator Wilhelm Maybach, 1846-1929. (DM.)

An interesting aerial view of a pair of Grosser W07 Mercedes Cabriolet Ds. Hitler stands in the front passenger section in the car at left. (Melin/HHA.)

The *Führer* gives the Nazi salute at a Hitler Youth rally in Berlin on May Day 1936 riding in a W07 *Offener*/Open Cabriolet D Touring Car. Facing him and returning the salute at center is HJ *Führer* Baldur von Schirach. (Melin/HHA.)

Nazi Propaganda Minister Dr. Josef Goebbels gives a back-handed casual Nazi salute (and *not* a wave) in W07 Cabriolet D Berlin license plate IA-III (his car) being followed by a Horch model car. (Melin/HHA.)

Dr. Gœbbels at Berlin Auto Show. (HHA)

German Air Force Commander-in-Chief Gen. Hermann Göring salutes the crowd from his Grosser W 07 Cabriolet D model "of late 1934 or 1935 production," license plate IIIA-33912, according to Melin. (Melin/HGA.)

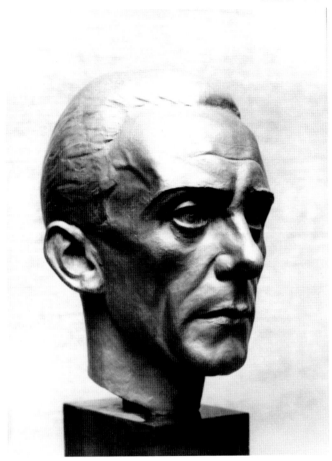

A bust sculpture of Nazi Propaganda Minister Dr. Paul Josef Gœbbels (1897-1945), possibly by sculptor Arno Breker. (Previously-unpublished photo, HHA.)

Göring again is in the front passenger seat as he leaves his personal Junkers Ju-52 transport aircraft, having returned to Berlin on October 20, 1934 from the funeral in Belgrade of the assassinated King Alexander of Yugoslavia. Göring's Air Force aide, Gen. Karl Bodenschatz, sits up front with the chauffeur, while in the rear seat are Göring (left) and his economic aide, Paul "Pilli" Körner. Note also the SS honor guard at the plane's tail, where appears as well both the Nazi swastika (right) and the famous Lufthansa German civilian airline logo. Noted Melin, the car is "Lacking external hood irons and with the artillery type wooden-spoked wheels on center-lock Rudge-Whitworth hubs." (Melin/HGA.)

King Farouk of Egypt salutes during a parade from his own W 07 Cabriolet D in 1938. He was overthrown after World War II by rebel Egyptian Army officers that included later Egyptian President Abdel Gamal Nasser. (Alain Dollfus, Paris.)

"Late series Grosser Mercedes W 07 Cabriolet F being prepared at the works for an exhibition," stated Melin. (Melin/MB.)

"A Grosser Mercedes W 07 Cabriolet F entered for the 1932 Wiesbaden Concurs d'Elegance," according to Jan Melin. (DB.)

"Hungarian Adm. Miklos Horthy (in rear seat) and wife visit Losonc in November 1938, traveling in their Grosser Mercedes W 07 Cabriolet D," noted Melin. (Gyula Buranyi.)

The Kaiser (left, wearing Uhlan helmet) and his initial First World War Chief of Imperial General Staff, Army Gen. Helmuth von Moltke the Younger, in His Majesty's wartime Mercedes, rear top down. (LC.)

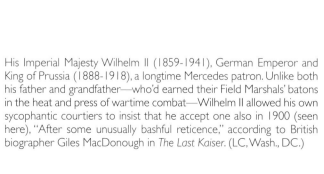

His Imperial Majesty Wilhelm II (1859-1941), German Emperor and King of Prussia (1888-1918), a longtime Mercedes patron. Unlike both his father and grandfather—who'd earned their Field Marshals' batons in the heat and press of wartime combat—Wilhelm II allowed his own sycophantic courtiers to insist that he accept one also in 1900 (seen here), "After some unusually bashful reticence," according to British biographer Giles MacDonough in *The Last Kaiser*. (LC, Wash., DC.)

"How to apply the Vigot lifting jack supplied with the Kaiser Wilhelm Grosser Mercedes W 07 Cabriolet F" license plate L-15237. (DB.)

Wearing Imperial Hohenzollern House livery, former race car driver Wilhelm Werner served as the Kaiser's personal driver during 1905-18, but did not go into His Majesty's Dutch exile that year. Note the emperor's personal pennant on the car at upper left. (LC.)

The Kaiser's chauffeur-in-exile was one Mr. Lange, seen here behind the wheel of his personal Cabriolet F W 07 model. Today the car is displayed at the famed Daimler-Benz Museum at Stüttgart, Germany. Note the sole Kompressor pipe on the right side of the engine, as well as the twin pennants mounted on the body's front section. (DB.)

His Majesty stops during an outing in Holland with his servants. He never returned to his native Prussia and Germany following his abdication in 1918. This is the same car as before. After his death on June 4, 1941, the car's rear section was modified to carry his coffin as a hearse. (Melin/ Frans Vrijaldenhoven.)

Reich Photo Reporter Prof. Heinrich Hoffmann (left) and Hitler (center) inspect a "Pre-production Grosser Mercedes W 150 Offener Tourenwagen intended for Hitler, and displayed at the 1938 Berlin Motor Show," noted Melin. (Melin/HHA.)

No wonder some observers thought that the car looked like it was "a city block long," as seen here during Hitler's April 20, 1939, birthday parade appearance in Berlin. Jan Melin calls this a "Pre-production or very early production Grosser Mercedes W 150 open touring car." Kempka drives, while the *Führer's* military adjutants ride behind them. The white-belted, black-coated SS troops at right are members of the *Führer's* own elite SSLAH bodyguard unit. (HHA.)

"Used by the Minister of Foreign Affairs [Joachim von Ribbentrop], this Grosser Mercedes W 150 Offener Tourenwagen (replacing a W 07) was photographed in late 1940," according to Melin. Note the pennant and wartime lamp covers in place. (Melin/JMA.)

Hitler enters his "Armored Grosser Mercedes W 150 Offener Tourenwagen in Berlin, 1943," most likely after the annual March Heroes' Memorial Day parade of the Armed Forces at this very location, outside the War Memorial Building. Shooting the weekly newsreel footage at left is the late *Luftwaffe* cameraman Walter Frentz, many of whose still color photos appear elsewhere in this book. (Alain Dollfus, Paris.)

"Same car with hood (top) raised, December 1941." (Melin/JMA.)

"Three W 150 Offener Tourenwagen, the one nearest to the camera with the hood (top) up being heavily armored. Note chrome trim spare wheel metal cover," stated Melin. (JMA.)

Another excellent view of the sheer *length* of these massive cars! Stated Melin, "A Grosser Mercedes W 150 Offener Tourenwagen in Austria, November 1940. Note the louvers on top of the bonnet (hood.)" (JMA.)

"The same car. Note the absence of over-riders on the bumpers," according to expert Jan Melin. (Alain Dollfus.)

"Grosser Mercedes W 150 Offener Tourenwagen in Krakow, Poland, 1942." (Alain Dollfus, Paris.)

"W 150 Offener Tourenwagen undergoing tests in the Stüttgart region," license plate IIIA-037. Note, too, the small, hooded lamp over the license plate at center. (Hermann Ahrens.)

"The same car now sporting Dutch license plates," asserted Melin, "on a visit to Switzerland, later reputedly being completely disassembled in The Netherlands." (Melin/JMA.)

Noted Melin, "Put at the disposal of Artur Seyss-Inquart in The Netherlands during the war, this W 150 Offener Tourenwagen was commandeered by the Americans in May 1945, and later this car was often seen with Prince Bernhard (of Holland) behind the wheel." Note, also, the U.S. Army's own white star emblazoned on the car's door. (Melin/JMA.)

Austrian Chancellor Artur Seyss-Inquart (fifth from right) and his Cabinet appear for a group photo after Hitler took Austria in March 1938. Ironically, later as the Reich Commissioner for Occupied Holland, Seyss served as Hitler's civil representative at the funeral of the former Kaiser, wherein the latter's Mercedes was converted to serve as His Majesty's hearse. (USNA.)

Stated Melin, "Commandeered in the Berchtesgaden region in 1945, this W 150 Offener Tourenwagen appears to be on a tow." (Alain Dollfus, Paris.)

Said Melin, "This Grosser Mercedes W 150 Pullman Limousine photographed in 1941 was owned by the works, but put at the disposal of the German Cabinet. Note the absence of chrome trim on the spare wheel metal cover. This was the actual car road tested by the British motoring magazine *The Motor* in May 1939." License plate IIIA-48003 with lamp covers and *Führerstandarte* affixed. (Melin/JMA.)

On November 19, 1940, Soviet People's Commissar of Foreign Affairs Vyacheslav M. Molotov was conveyed from Berlin's Anhalter train station to the New German Reich Chancellery in Berlin via "This armored W 150 Pullman Limousine," noted Melin. Seen here, the car pulls up at the NRC's main doorway on the spacious Honor Courtyard as two servants stand ready to assist at left and an honor guard of Hitler's own elite SSLAH bodyguard unit presents arms to Molotov at right rear. He reentered this same area in July 1945 as a guest of the Red Army. (Joachim von Ribbentrop Albums, USNA, College Park, MD.)

Molotov (left)—called "Old Stone Ass" by his former chief, Lenin—meets with Hitler (right) in the latter's spacious private office sitting area within the NRC on November 19, 1940. The breakdown of these talks convinced the Nazi *Führer* at last that he must invade the USSR, as he did so on June 22, 1941. Between them here sits the German Foreign Office interpreter Dr. Gustav Hilger. (JRA.)

Stated Melin, "Grosser Mercedes W 150 Pullman Limousine, probably chassis number 189779, used in 1945 by French Air Minister Charles Tillon." (Alain Dollfus, Paris.)

"Grosser Mercedes W 150 Pullman Limousine, chassis number 150006/0003, commandeered in the Obersalzberg region and here being demonstrated in Paris in 1945..." (Alain Dollfus, Paris.)

"...and being exhibited in Paris." (Alain Dollfus, Paris.)

Norwegian rightist leader Vidkun Quisling (left) greets German RFSS Heinrich Himmler (right) during the latter's visit during the war. (CER.)

Stated Melin, "Two photos showing one of only 10 produced armored W 150 Innenlenkers, this one being used by Quisling in Norway during the war, chassis number 150006/0018." The photos were taken outside the Oslo Police Headquarters in May 1945. Quisling was shot by the Norwegians after the war. British POW Himmler committed suicide by taking cyanide poison during interrogation on May 23, 1945. (Melin.)

Hitler enters the Berlin Olympic Stadium in 1936 for the start of the Summer Games riding in an "Experimental W 24 Offener Tourenwagen, followed by a Grosser Mercedes W 07," according to Melin. The stadium still stands today. (HHA.)

Left: The very same car, but with its convertible top up. What the *Führer's* security men are doing at left is not clear to the author. (Alain Dollfus, Paris, HHA.) **Right:** "The Experimental Type W 24 with the 5.4-liter straight-8 engine," said Melin. "Note that the vent shutters in the bonnet (hood)-side are open." Hitler and Kempka are in front, with an unidentified SS man sitting just behind them on a mid-car jump seat at left, and SS Gen. Julius Schaub sitting at right mid-car. Alone in the rear seat is Propaganda Minister Dr. Josef Gœbbels. This is license plate 1A-103708. (Alain Dollfus, Paris/HHA.)

A company ad from the 1930s reads: "The Mercedes-Benz Star—in the whole world a symbol of design peak performance, conscientiousness, meticulous materials, and careful craftsmanship." (DBM.)

The enduring image from 1909-2009. The former laurel wreath around the star—used from the merger of Daimler and Benz in 1926—was dropped in 1937, and this has been the symbol ever since. (DBM.)

Various samples of company-sponsored artwork follow; first, of the famous three-pointed star logo adopted in 1909. According to Beverly Rae Kimes, "At first, both a three-pointed and a four-pointed star were used, but the latter was soon dropped. From 1911-16, there were variations to the surround of the star, which bore the name of the factory of origin, either Untertürkheim or Marienfeld. It was in 1909 that the two accents [over the double e] were dropped from the name Mercedes. From 1916-22, the large three-pointed star was surrounded by a band containing miniature three-pointed stars." (DBM.)

A beautiful example of the company-sponsored artwork of Hans Liska (1907-83) from his work *The Auto and Fashion*. One of the world's great automotive artists, Liska was born in Vienna in 1907, the son of a shoemaker and a female butcher. His first drawings were in their basement, using coal on its walls. After attending the Vienna Arts and Crafts School, young Liska went to work in an advertising agency in Switzerland, then managed an art studio in Zurich, where he also took language lessons from the famous Irish poet and author James Joyce. (DBM.)

The Daimler-Benz central administrative buildings in Stüttgart, Germany, in the shadow of the three-pointed star, by Liska from his work *The Auto and Fashion*. After attending another arts and crafts school, Liska had a piece of his art published by Ulstein's *Berlin Illustrated Magazine* in its New Year's issue of 1932-33 as the back cover, and thus he got his start. He'd gone to Berlin on May 1, 1932, and in time covered many famous people: Mussolini, the Pope, and the King of England, to mention but a few. (Roger Wychgram Collection, Aberdeen, MD.)

An earlier Mercedes logo. The Benz trademark was a laurel wreath. Here is an interesting anecdote from mechanic Charlie Stitch of Grand Gorge, NY, as told to authors Victor Boesin and Wendy Grad for their work *The Mercedes-Benz Book*: "A Mercedes was the first car he ever rode in...'My car was a showpiece wherever it went.'...On the front seat rested a three-pointed star radiator ornament. 'We used to put these things on the hood, on the front of the radiator, any part of the car it would show up best. I devised the idea of making a ring around the star and a stand to carry it on the radiator cap. I wanted to make the star more eye-catching. Your eyes see the large ring first...Up to that time, all they had was the star.'" "The points of the star were sharpened in 1927, and Charlie's ring-around-the-star emblem logo was reportedly seen by the New York Mercedes dealer. "I used to park at the Mercedes showrooms at 56th and Broadway. In about 1927, Mercedes cars from the factories began to carry the emblem on the radiator cap." (DBM.)

Company artwork by Mercedes artist Hans Liska, wherein a toddler grins from the front seat of a Mercedes-Benz open touring car from *The Auto and Fashion*. After the war, Liska was briefly a farm laborer, married wife Liesl, and had daughter Angelika. He returned to commercial artwork as a Ford Motor Company artist. The German Mühlens firm in Cologne then established a 25-year relationship with him. (Roger Wychgram Collection, Aberdeen, MD.)

"Horsepower under the hood," a clever concept by artist Hans Liska from *The Auto and Fashion*. In 1950 Liska started drawing brochures and posters for the Daimler-Benz Company, and this led to his resignation from Ford. Among his many Mercedes projects was a book of pictures and funny drawings that was distributed to both workers and customers. After Daimler ended its racing circuit participation in 1955, Liska switched from books back to posters and brochures, and also did freelance work for other German firms, such as Hoescht, and Marklin. The current author represented American Hoescht Plastics for Emery Advertising of Hunt Valley, MD, during the 1980s. (Roger Wychgram Collection, Aberdeen, MD.)

A company ad showing its production decline under the Weimar Republic from 1928-32, and then growth during the Third Reich into 1935—way up. In 1939, Liska was drafted into the German Army as a propaganda company artist covering the German side of World War II, having some of his work published in the wartime picture magazine *Signal*. His first picture book—*Junkers Plane and Motor Works*—was published in 1942. A later volume—*The War Sketch Books, 1939-42*—was published in the latter year. (DBM.)

Stated author Frederic Spotts in his excellent study *Hitler and the Power of Aesthetics*, "Hitler's portrait is displayed in a Mercedes automobile showroom in Münich in 1935. From the early days of the Nazi movement, Hitler traveled in a large, open Mercedes. After Hitler came to power, Mercedes hoped to cash in on the long-standing association in the public mind between Hitler and the car company. The message is: Buy a Mercedes and you will be driving the Führer's car," an image that the company ever since 1945 has gone to extraordinary lengths to *downplay*, right up to this moment of writing in 2009. The portrait itself is also of interest, as it depicts Hitler wearing the "Führer uniform" that he began using in August 1934 after the death of his then nominal superior, Reich President and Field Marshal Paul von Hindenburg. (DBM.)

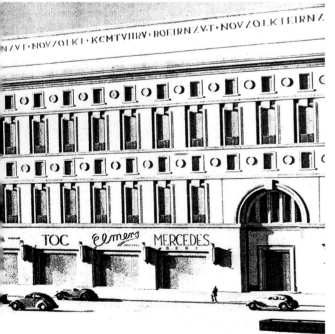

The model of an office building for Berlin's planned North-South Axis road to be built by Hitler architect Albert Speer for the capital's transformation to the new *Germania* by 1950—after Nazi Germany had won the Second World War. The model was by architect Gotthold Nestler, and features a Mercedes showroom on the ground floor at center. Often drawing 10-12 hours daily, Liska used the following media in his work: India ink, chalk, coal, pencil, water colors, and oils applied by brush, sponge, fingers, and even handkerchiefs! A 1983 exhibition of his multifaceted work at the Daimler-Benz Museum at Stüttgart—attended by the artist—preceded his death of a heart attack that December 26th. (DBM.)

The DaimlerChryler Museum logo more recently. (Courtesy Maria Feifel, DBM.)

As I wrote in 1999, "Hitler at the very apex of his glory, July 6, 1940, in license plate IA-148461. The left backup RSD car is license plate IIA-19356, of Münich registry, while the right-hand car is license plate Pol 38751, a Police car. All three lead vehicles are Grosser Mercedes W 150 open tourers." Noted fellow author Aaron L. Johnson in his 2001 work *Hitler's Military Headquarters: Organization, Structures, Security, and Personnel,* "Hitler's return to his capital after the brilliantly successful campaign in the West, was a great personal triumph for him. The streets of Berlin between the railroad station and the Chancellery on the Wilhelmsplatz were packed with cheering Berliners. The streets were covered with flowers, and all of the church bells of Berlin rang." Later, this same Mercedes-Benz Grosser 770K was on display in the Imperial Palace Auto Museum Collection at Las Vegas, NV. Note the headlamp covers with their nighttime driving slits, and the two back-up cars of Reich Security Service (RSD) men. (HHA.)

Robert Bosch (1861-1942): from ignition to headlamps. German inventor and electrical engineer Robert Bosch did his first work for Daimler on magnetos. From ignitions in 1911, Bosch went on to other electrical components, such as Daimler's first headlamp assembly, made in 1913, the same year as Rudolf Diesel's suicide. Bosch was also the first to place a horn inside a car, in 1921. According to *The German Millenium*, "Robert Bosch was a highly successful industrialist and an extraordinary man. He was the founder of a 'workshop for fine mechanics' in Stüttgart in 1896. The factory prospered and the company became public in 1916." (DBM.)

"The 70-year-old Robert Bosch stands proudly in front of his company's stand at the Berlin Automobile Exhibition in 1931. Bosch had produced the first lamps for motor cars in the days of Daimler and Benz, and was the still the leading company in this area," attested *The German Millenium*. "Suddenly and shockingly, the world around him changed. Bosch lived on till March 12, 1942, when he died in Stüttgart. He was spared the worst; that was yet to come." (DBM.)

Chancellor Hitler (center, right) is greeted by German Defense (later War) Minister Army Gen. Werner von Blomberg, whom Hitler later named as the Third Reich's first Field Marshal. Note the Bosch headlamps on the Grosser at far right, with the unusual license plate Z-57501. Continues *The German Millenium*, "Bosch was condemned by rivals for his supposedly 'Red' or Socialist views. He introduced an eight-hour working day for his employees in 1906—an almost unheard of practice at that time." (HHA.)

An excellent view of a pair of pristine Bosch headlamps, with Hitler and Gœbbels (wearing white motoring cap) studying a road map. Note, too, that the windshield is folded down. (HHA.)

Grosser license plate IIA-19357 with Hitler and Schreck up front and Julius Schaub on the mid-car jump seat behind Schreck. Behind their vehicle can be seen the first SS/RSD security car, with its occupants riding on the side running boards. (HHA.)

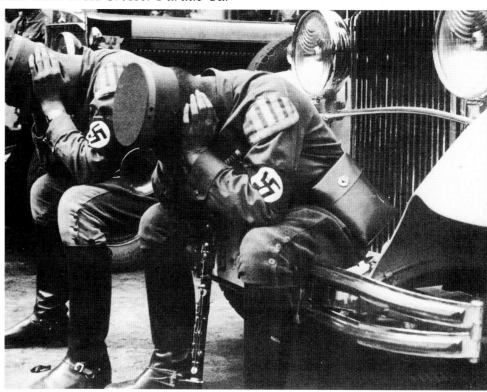

Weary SA bandsmen rest their heads in their hands while sitting on the front bumper of a cars. Note the pennants on the car at left, and also the traditional "birdcage" shoulder pads on the uniforms. Pride of place, however, goes to the Bosch headlamps at upper right! (HHA.)

An excellent view of the Grosser's complete complement of covered lamps of all sizes on license plate IA-148656. The wartime covers had slits that emitted a small shaft of light onto the road ahead for nighttime driving to protect the car's occupants from Allied air attacks, an increasingly dangerous problem after 1942. (DBM.)

Hitler salutes German factory workers on a wartime visit. Note that all the wartime headlamp covers are in place, as well as the Nazi Party pennant on the right front mudguard. Kempka is at the wheel, while *Reichsleiter/National Leader* Martin Bormann (left) and SS Gen. Julius Schaub (right) are in the rear seating area. (HHA.)

This is the Grosser that is today on display at the Canadian War Museum at Ottawa, Ontario, Canada. Here, SS valet Heinz Linge prepares to open the right front door for the *Führer* to get out and enter the Berlin Kroll Opera House on July 19, 1940, to address the *Reichstag* after the successful 1940 Western campaign. The car is a W 150 open tourer and has all its lamp covers in place. Army adjutant Maj. Rudolf Schmundt (left) and SS Gen. Julius Schaub (right) are exiting the car at center, while gray-clad SSLAH men line the curb for security for the *Führer's* grand entrance, with Regular German police behind them. SS Gen. Sepp Dietrich paces at the far left. (HHA.)

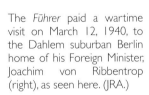

The *Führer* paid a wartime visit on March 12, 1940, to the Dahlem suburban Berlin home of his Foreign Minister, Joachim von Ribbentrop (right), as seen here. (JRA.)

Hungarian Regent Adm. Miklos Horthy (second from left) and Schaub (left) leave a train station in East Prussia for an August 1941 visit to Hitler's headquarters as Linge (center, back to camera) holds open the waiting Grosser's door at right. Note the lamp covers. (HHA.)

The visit over, the *Führer* departs, entering his open tourer as Linge holds open the door for him at left. Note the small lamp cover. (Previously-unpublished photo from the Joachim von Ribbentrop Albums, USNA, College Park, MD.)

Hitler's car and SS/RSD escort vehicle about to pull away from the curb of von Ribbentrop's Dahlem home. Ribbentrop salutes from the top of the driveway steps at left, while Hitler is in the front seat beside the chauffeur, where he almost always rode. Behind Hitler sits his adjutant in *Waffen*/Armed SS uniform, Julius Schaub, and next to him is *Luftwaffe* adjutant Col. Nikolaus von Below. Between Hitler and Schaub sits an SS escort officer. Note the lamp covering with nighttime driving slit. The occasion is von Ribbentrop's birthday. (Previously-unpublished photo, JRA.)

A good lateral view of a Grosser showing hub wheel covers, spare tire mount, *Führerstandarte*, honeycomb radiator, and all frontal lamps with covers affixed. Hitler sits in front, with Linge behind him on the mid-car jump seat. (HHA.)

Hitler's Grosser at the March 1943 Heroes' Memorial Day observance in Berlin. Hitler and Kempka are in front with an unknown man in the left mid-car jump seat, von Below in the right, and Schaub at right rear. Note the lamp covers and Nazi Party pennant at right front on the mudguard. (HHA.)

Two close-up views of the *Führerstandarte/Leader Standard* on the right front fenders of Hitler's cars, its placement when he was the ranking person present in the vehicles. When foreign Heads of State or Prime Ministers were present as guests, their pennants flew in that location instead, and his was assigned to the left fender. Note also the three-pointed radiator star ornaments and the Bosch headlamps. (HHA.)

License plate IA-103708 as it was displayed after the war, with *Führerstandarte* and Nazi Party flags affixed. Note also the Bosch headlamps and the emplaced bulletproof side windows. (LC.)

The *Führer* strides to his waiting 770K Grosser, his height providing some scale to the size of the *Führerstandarte* and silver pipe at left on the car. He is leaving the memorial service in Berlin at St. George's Church for the deceased British King George V in 1936. (HHA.)

A good frontal-side view of the Grosser arriving at a stadium, plus an excellent view of the car's chrome accoutrements. Hitler and Kempka are up front, with German Army C-in-C Gen. Walther von Brauchitsch at left rear and German Navy chief Adm. Dr. Erich Raeder at right. (HHA.)

The *Führer* (center) shakes hands with HJ Leader Baldur von Schirach at the September 1935 Nürnberg Party Congress at center as his SS bodyguard Karl Wilhelm Krause (left) prepares to open his passenger door and Schreck is at the wheel, with the *Führerstandarte* visible. Note the man at right with the small stepladder—for a photographer. (HHA.)

A typical wartime 770K Berghof departure. Eva Braun is coming up the front steps, while Heinz Linge—with Hitler's light raincoat over his left arm—sees to it that the *Führer* is well-seated next to Kempka. Martin Bormann is seated at left rear next to Hitler's Naval adjutant, Capt. Karl-Jesko von Puttkammer. (Eva Braun Hitler Albums, USNA, College Park, MD.)

A good view of the top of the spare wheel cover as Hitler shares a laugh with Göring (left), who wears SA brown uniform and cap. Between them stands Göring's Air Force aide, Gen. Karl Bodenschatz, who survived the war and them both. Interior Minister Wilhelm Frick stands between Bodenschatz and Hitler at rear, and to the far right is Rudolf Hess, also wearing SA togs. SA Chief of Staff Viktor Lütze is at far left. (HHA.)

The *Führerstandarte* is just visible at the left on the Grosser. Hitler (center) shakes hands with Göring, who wears both Air Force uniform and a flowing *Lufwtaffe* blue cape emblazoned with an eagle on the left. Just in front of the car's grill—looking at the two men—is Nazi Education Minister Bernhard Rust, and between him and Hitler, coming down the steps, is the *Führer's* SA adjutant during 1923-40, Gen. Wilhelm Brückner. Next to him at right is Göring's aide, Paul "Pilli" Körner, and Gen. Bodenschatz can be seen standing on the step just to the right of Göring. (HHA.)

From left to right: German Army Field Marshal Wilhelm Keitel—Chief of the High Command of the Armed Forces—King Boris of Bulgaria, and Hitler's NSKK (Nazi Motor Korps) adjutant, Albert Bormann, younger brother of Martin Bormann. The scene is at Hitler's principal wartime military *Führer* Headquarters, *Wolfsschanze/Wolf's Lair*, at Rastenburg, East Prussia, during the winter of 1941-42. Note the *Führerstandarte* being covered at left with its leather hood by the unknown officer, possibly chauffeur Erick Kempka. (HHA.)

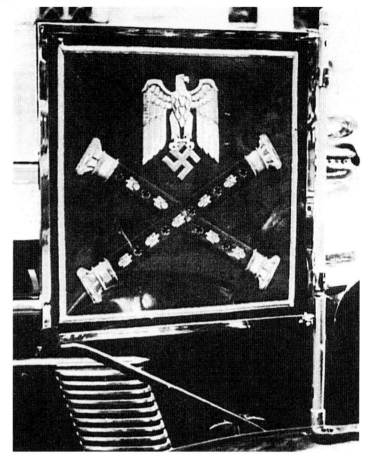

The motor vehicle pennant for an Army General Field Marshal that was brought into service on April 21, 1941, during the German Balkans Campaign that conquered Greece and Yugoslavia. (CER.)

A good view of a British Union Jack car pennant at left on one of the cars used by Great Britain's Prime Minister Neville Chamberlain and his suite when they visited the German Chancellor at the Dreesen Hotel in Godesberg, on the Rhine River, in September 1938 during the Czech Crisis. Hitler stands at center at the hotel's main entrance, about to shake his guest's hand. To the right of Hitler is German Foreign Office interpreter Dr. Paul Schmidt. At left is photographer Heinrich Hoffmann, and next to him von Ribbentrop. On the steps above them at center is Keitel. (HHA.)

Lineup of staff cars with various pennants affixed. (CER.)

During the Fall 1935 military maneuvers, a roadside conference is held by, from left to right: an unknown German Army general, defense Minister Werner von Blomberg, Chancellor Hitler, and Army C-in-C Gen. Werner von Fritsch. Note the officers with the white hatbands, maneuver judges for the annual war games. At right is parked a Mercedes-Cabriolet 320 open tourer, but for our purposes here note the pennant of the War Minister affixed. (HHA.)

Not a Grossser, but note the pennant: "The diagonally quartered red, white, and black emblem for a commanding general painted directly onto a metal plate and carried fitted into a metal frame on the wing of a staff car," according to one source. (CER.)

During Hitler's September 1939 wartime tours of conquered Poland, he used a vehicle other than his standard G-4 cross-country cars on at least one occasion, as seen here. At center, RSD commander Johann Rattenhuber bawls out an order to clear the way for the *Führer*, who stands in an Army staff open tourer car, its pennant seen on the mudguard at right. (HHA.)

A previously-unpublished photo of Hitler in an Army staff car, either in Poland 1939 or Russia 1941. He sits in the front seat, with the Army pennant visible at right. (HHA.)

RFSS Heinrich Himmler enters a *Luftwaffe* staff car with pennant affixed. States American author G.L. Sweeting, he is "Escorted by a *Luftwaffe* general, commander of a *Luftgau/Air Force District*, as shown by the flag on the fender. The 'WL' on the license plate indicates *Wehrmacht-Luftwaffe/Armed Forces Air Force*. Other military vehicles can be identified by 'WH,' which stands for Armed Forces Army, while 'WM' meant Armed Forces Navy. The license numbers on SS vehicles were preceded by the SS runes." Accurate on all counts! (Sweeting.)

According to writer Gregory Douglas in his article *Command Flags of the CIC and Chief of the Wehrmacht, 1935-45* in the Fall 1993 issue of *The Military Advisor*, "On March 14, 1933, a new flag was instituted for the Reich War Minister, replacing the Weimar Republic issue. This flag consisted of a white square bordered with the re-instituted national colors of black (top), white, and red (bottom) with a superimposed Iron Cross..." (Roger Bender.)

"It was replaced on July 23, 1935 with a new issue that represented the amalgamation of the offices of the Reich War Minister and the Commander-in-Chief of the Wehrmacht. The center device was identical, but reduced in size on a white background, and the edging was black-white-black. In each corner of the flag were black Wehrmacht eagles, heads towards the center, and facing right. A very short-lived flag, it was cancelled and replaced on Oct. 5, 1935 with an entirely different model based on the new Reich War Flag." (Roger Bender.)

"The official regulations stated that, 'The flag of the Reich War Minister and CIC Wehrmacht is the War Flag with the following changes: 'The flag is in the form of a square with a black and white border. In the upper left and lower right corners are Iron Crosses and in the lower right and upper left are Wehrmacht eagles.' The orders further stated that the flag was authorized for use on naval units, aircraft, buildings, vehicles, and small boats. When (Field Marshal Werner von) Blomberg resigned his offices in 1938, Adolf Hitler became the CIC Wehrmacht, and Gen. Wilhelm Keitel became the Chief of the Wehrmacht High Command, or Chief of the Oberkommando der Wehrmacht (OKW), a post he held until the end of the war." (Roger Bender.)

"On Aug. 6, 1938, a new flag was authorized for this latter position, and consisted of a pennant form with a black outer and white inner border, a red field, with the War Flag swastika in the center." (Roger Bender.)

Second pattern pennant for the Chief of the *Wehrmacht* featuring twin crossed Army Field Marshal batons. (Chizar/Roger Bender.)

SA flag, "To be used from May 1, 1935." (Philippe Gillair/Roger Bender.)

Not a Grosser. "The similarity between the SS pattern and the SA form is evident in this photograph of SA *Gruppenführer*/Group Leader Karl Ernst (left, saluting) during a ride through Berlin. On the right fender, the 1932 pattern SA car flag for SA Group Berlin-Brandenburg is flown. The SA had a group designation, and the SS an Oberabschnitt one since early 1934. Note the October 1933 pattern Prussian State car flag (which was also a police pattern) on the left fender. This was permitted, as Ernst was as Prussian Staatsrat/State official. Note the use of a large SA trumpet banner for Storm 5/2 for the Berlin district of Schöneberg by the individual standing on the left running board." (Otto Spronk/Roger Bender.)

"Command flag with proper national colors. J. Wotka Collection. Blocher File." (Roger Bender.)

"Command Flag was used as Staff ID for Police Regiment 9, Riga, Latvia, October 1942, Wotka Collection, Kamman File." (Roger Bender.)

Not a Grosser: "Command Flag of Commander of Police Regiment Mahren/Moravia, Czech Protectorate, 1940. Dr. Werner Regenberg Collection." (Roger Bender.)

Above: "Illustrated are the pole top patterns used by the SS. Only the circle with eagle was the official type as described in the 1933 and 1936 regulations for use with the higher ranked car flags. Whether the eagle version from 1936 was to have pointed or angular wings is not mentioned." (W.P.B.R Saris/Roger Bender.)

Left: "Car flag with black fields, as used by the Reichsführer/National Administrator SS. The side—as with all flag drawings— is the official 'front.' The RFSS pattern was copied from the SA Obergruppe flag, which was introduced on Sept. 25, 1932. Drawn by W.P.B.R. Saris." (Roger Bender.)

Not a Grosser. "Command flag of Police Battalion 131 Wilna Poland, 1941. J. Wotka Collection." (Roger Bender.)

"The RFSS car flag is positioned on the wrong fender of a car from the Berlin district in this 1936 photograph," the year when Himmler was named by Hitler as national Chief of the German Police. "The flag has an eagle pole top with no outer ring. On the right fender, where officially this flag was to be positioned, is an empty pole with the same eagle. This Himmler car flag has the 1933 pattern eagle." (Jeff Hammond/Roger Bender.)

Not Grossers. "The SS Group Staff pattern car flag for Oberabschnitt Middle was flown on two occasions in 1934. The photo at right was taken at Halle during the inauguration of the new leader for Standard 26, and Oberabschnitt leader Heike. The above photo was taken in June 1934 at Dresden where Standard 46 was located. On the right fender, the Group Staff flag is flown, while the square SS Standard Staff pattern is positioned on the left fender. The word Mitte/Middle is slightly visible in the photo. Later, both Standards were located in Oberabschnitt Elbe." (Jost W. Schenider/Roger Bender.)

Not a Grossser. "Command flag with colored cover, not authorized when displaying flag. Photo from Gerald Stezelberger." (Roger Bender.)

"This pennant was used on all forms of vehicles by members of the SS. Note that the SS runes were not positioned within a circle yet," as occurred later. "SS Wimpel/SS Pennant. From late 1933, simple pennants were flown by SS members from their cars, motorcycles, and bicycles...Another authorized form was red, with a swastika within the central white circle. The red pennant was topped with an eagle emblem within a circle, or a swastika within a circle. The red pennant used by the SS most often piped along the two longest side in black/white." (Roger Bender.)

Not a Grosser. "From late 1933, simple pennants could be flown by SS members on cars, motorcycles, and even bicycles. This vehicle from the Thuringen area shows the use of a black pennant with large SS runes on the right fender. The pennant is framed." (David Delich/Roger Bender.)

2

The "*Chauffeureska*"
Hitler's Driver/Bodyguards and the *Kampfzeit*

Emil Maurice, 1897-1972

Emil Maurice joined the early German Workers' Party (forerunner of the later Nazi Party) in 1919. Having taken part in the failed November 8-9, 1923, Beer hall *Putsch*/Revolt, Maurice was sent with Hitler, Hess, and others to Landsberg Prison, outside Münich. After his release, he became one of Hitler's earliest known driver-bodyguards, an inner circle that eventually became known within Party circles as the *Führer's* "*Chauffeuereska*," a term later expanded to include *all* of Hitler's inner circle: secretaries, aides, adjutants, guards, cooks, barbers, etc. They were an important part of both his daily regimen and regime, in that they served to make Hitler an effective Nazi Chief Executive Officer, or CEO in American corporate terms.

As I wrote in *Apex of Glory* in 2006, "In 1935, Maurice—now an SS *Standartenführer*/ Colonel and Münich City Councilor—applied for permission to the SS to get married. It was found by the SS department for Aryan Ancestrage that Maurice was partly Jewish. Heinrich Himmler, head of the SS, told Hitler; however, Hitler was unwilling to purge his old friend from the NSDAP/Nazi Party and SS.

"Maurice actually continued to receive promotions within the SS, and remained as a Münich City Councilor. He survived the war, and was sentenced by a de-Nazification court to four years in a labor camp."

In her excellent 1985 study, *The SA: An Historical Perspective*, authoress Jill Halcomb confirmed that the then 23-year-old Maurice was the first commander of the SA, adding, "Maurice became Hitler's chauffeur after leaving the SA." As to the 1935 marriage incident, author Charles Hamilton added, "At this time he was an SS Colonel... Maurice and his bride had to submit proof of Aryan origin before they could wed....

"In the words of Heinrich Himmler, 'Without question, SS *Standartenführer* Emil Maurice is, according to his ancestral table, not of Aryan decent.' Hitler refused, however, to purge Maurice from the SS or the Party. Himmler was outraged over this, but the debacle did not hurt Maurice's career significantly' by 1939 he had been promoted to SS Brigadier General, and remained a Ratsherr City Councillor of Münich."

"Before Hitler's birthday parade on Apr. 20, 1936, which took place on the Charlottenburger Chaussee, Hitler reviews the assembled troops," from author Horst Scheibert's 1997 work *Parades of the Wehrmacht: Berlin, 1934-40*. This is an extremely rare picture for two main reasons: first, Hitler gives the Nazi salute from a sitting position while in a moving car. Second, this is one of the last times he was driven by his chauffeur of a decade, Julius Schreck, who died less than a month later. Note, too, that the windshield of license plate #11A-19356 is in the down position. Also note the lined up *Panzerwagen* I tanks at left. (HHA.)

Thus, Hitler passed over a second chance to get even with his former chauffeur over the Geli Raubal affair—in which, allegedly, the two men had both been her lovers—but chose not to. Loyalty for past services—such as taking part in the June 30, 1934, Blood Purge against the SA—it seems won out over jealousy, and a desire for revenge.

Indeed, when the *Führer's* plane landed at Münich airfield at 4 AM on Saturday, June 30, 1934, Hitler discovered that Maurice had been among those Nazi stalwarts who had already arrested the Münich SA leaders. In his biography of Hitler, German author Konrad Heiden reported that Maurice led a murder gang that shot three times in the heart and broke the neck of Father Bernhard Stempfle, a Catholic priest who'd helped edit *Mein Kampf/My Battle*, and also "knew too much" of Geli's death.

In 2001, there appeared the landmark biography by German author Lothar Machtan entitled *The Hidden Hitler*, which made a very strong case that Hitler was a homosexual and that, indeed, so were most of his top Nazi Party associates. My own view is that Hitler was bisexual. Machtan added another dimension to the lives of Emil Maurice and his successor as chauffeur, Julius Schreck.

Machtan called Maurice, "The high-spirited daredevil to whom he (Hitler) became increasingly attached. Maurice received his first public accolade in January 1922, when Hitler enthusiastically referred to him as 'our greyhound.' On that occasion, the Party leader was recalling a public brawl in the Hofbrauhaus (beer hall in Münich), which he later described as the SA's 'babtism of fire.' It was then, in November 1921, that he had been instantly struck by the slim young man's vigorous and pugnacious appearance.

"Born near Eckenforde in 1897, Maurice had trained as a watchmaker in his native North Germany before moving to Münich in 1917. After World War I, in which he saw a few months' military service, he became politically active. In 1919, he joined Hitler's Party, and before long he was commanding its 'Gymnastic and Sports Section'—in other words, the bouncers who saw off political opponents at public meetings.

"At some stage in 1921, he became Hitler's chauffeur and, thus, one of his closest associates. That he was now one of the intimates is confirmed by Julius Schaub, who described Maurice after the war as the man who 'probably knew more than anyone else about Hitler's early days up to 1925.' Together with Hitler's 'Assault Squad,' he took part in the November 1923 *Putsch/Revolt*, was duly convicted, and served his sentence at Landsberg from April 1924 until the end of January 1925.

"While there, he acted as Hitler's liaison officer and confidential agent, dealt with his correspondence, and produced the fair copy of his *Mein Kampf* manuscript" (along with Hess.)...In 1926, when Gœbbels encountered his boss 'in mountain dress' (lederhosen), he commented: 'Looks quite droll.' Hitler evidently liked his North German chauffeur to wear this quaint get-up.

"At Landsberg—if not before—the two men became close friends. Hitler called Maurice 'Maurizl' or 'Mosel;' Maurice addressed the 'Führer' simply as 'my dear Hitler,' a very self assured form of address for a henchman eight years younger and without any political services to his name....

"In the years that followed, Hitler granted his chauffeur access to the innermost reaches of his private life. Maurice had a key to Hitler's Thierschstrasse lodgings (in Münich), took care of his clothes and laundry, and performed many other mundane chores that would normally have been undertaken by a housekeeper.

"But Maurice was also there when things got tough, and never shirked a fight—something for which Hitler officially commended his 'good Maurice.' As an automobile fan, Hitler took a special delight in Maurice's driving. They 'always zoomed along at top speed,' Rudolf Hess recalled later. 'Maurice, supercharger!'—that was how we used to race around.'"

But Maurice—unlike Hitler generally—was also attracted to women as well as men. "The Führer himself discovered handsome Emil's sentimental secret. He dismissed the matter with a forgiving smile." As a cover for their joint homosexuality, the two men often went "trolling for girls" around Münich's nighttime bars, clubs, and cafes—with Hitler giving the girls money, but nothing else.

Hitler fired Maurice over the Geli Raubal liaison at Christmas 1927, and the following April 1928 Maurice took his former boss to court over payment of back pay owed, and won his case. On August 1, 1928, Hitler paid off Maurice with 20,000 RM in hush money.

"He now quit the stage. Although he did not leave the Party, he and Hitler were through...When the National Socialists (Nazis) came to power in the spring of 1933, Emil Maurice reentered his 'dear Hitler's' service," Machtan asserts...Maurice further stated that he had approached Hitler in person 'with deep concern'" about Himmler. "As luck would have it, Hitler had immediately shaken hands 'in token of reconciliation,' and told him: "Mosel, I did you an injustice.'"

On March 9, 1933, the day that the Nazis took complete political power in Bavaria, Maurice joined Hitler's publisher Max Amann in storming the offices of a rival political newspaper and assaulting its editor, for which Hitler secured Maurice's appointment to the Münich City Council. After taking part in the June 30, 1934 Blood Purge against the SA, Maurice was appointed an SS *Standartenfuher*/Colonel.

"In October 1934, Maurice was invited by Hitler to join him on an excursion to Landsberg, and he was also present at the annual commemoration of the Münich *Putsch*... It transpired after the war that the two men were not only reconciled, but on friendly terms once more: Maurice's de-Nazification papers record that he was Hitler's 'constant companion' whenever the latter came to stay in Münich, and his attorney conceded that 'The Führer liked to see him when present in Münich.'

"From now on, Hitler was unstinting with his solicitous gestures of friendship. In 1935, when Maurice decided to marry a medical student 14 years younger than himself, Hitler attended their engagement party at the Hotel *Vierjahreszeiten/Four Seasons*. 'He was extremely charming to me,' Hedwig Maurice recalled later: 'Not a practiced charm, but one that comes from the heart.' It was ostentatiously announced that the Führer was making his apartment available for the forthcoming wedding reception. Although Hitler had to cry off at short notice, he visited the newlyweds' new home soon afterward, and made them a wedding gift of 1,000 RM."

When Himmler tried to kick Maurice out of the SS, "Hitler ruled that, 'In this one, exceptional case,' Maurice and his brothers could remain in the SS 'because he was his very first companion, and he and his brothers and the whole Maurice family had served with rare courage and devotion during the Movement's earliest and most difficult months and years.'"

Concluded Machtan, "It was remarkable, the treatment to which Hitler subjected Emil Maurice within the space of 10 years: affection, condemnation, compromise, rehabilitation, protection. There are two possible explanations for these abrupt ups and downs. Either Hitler had never stopped loving his 'greyhound,' all disappointments and irritations notwithstanding, or he was so afraid of him that it seemed wiser to bribe him than risk the imponderable results of liquidating him. Once again, the truth probably lies midway between the two."

I concur, and add that these "ups and downs" have all the classic earmarks of homosexual lovers' spats, complete with "kiss and makeup."

Julius Schreck, 1898-1936

As I wrote in *Apex of Glory* in 2006, "Having set up a new bodyguard unit—the *Schutzstaffel* or SS in 1925—Schreck (born July 13, 1898) gave over control to Josef Berchtold, after he returned from Austria. Schreck then took on the role of Hitler's chauffeur, succeeding Emil Maurice. Schreck was well liked by all those who met him.

"Hitler held him in particularly high regard. Hitler stated, 'Schreck is the best driver you can imagine, and our supercharger is good for over a hundred! We always drive very fast, but in recent times, I've told Schreck not to go over 50.' In 1942, Hitler recalled a journey back to Münich from Mainz in the late 1920s.

"'We arrived in the middle of a bunch of cyclists. They were Reds, and began to hurl insults at us, but when they heard Schreck sounding a siren, they left their bicycles on the road and scattered into the fields. Schreck went by quite calmly, crushing the bicycles. The Reds were taken aback, wondering how a police car could behave like that! When they realized their mistake, they began to abuse us again in their choicest terms: 'Murderers! Bandits! Hitlerites!'

"'They recognized me, and I take that fact as my badge of rank. We often had very painful incidents of this kind. It was no joke, at that time, to find oneself at grips with a mob of opponents.'

"Hitler also mentioned that, 'Theoretical and practical knowledge are one thing, and presence of mind at the moment of danger is something else. Schreck had them both to the same degree. He was strong as a buffalo, and cold-bloodedly fearless. He would use his car as a weapon against the Communists. How terrible if something had happened to me!'"

In 1931, during a heated argument with leftist Nazi Party rival leader Otto Strasser, Hitler yelled out, "I would not allow my chauffeur to eat worse than myself!" in defending the socialist part of his brand of Nazism.

SS man and chauffeur Julius Schreck was not only the *Führer's* principal driver for over a decade, but he was also a major figure in the origins and development of both the SA and the SS. He was Nazi Party member #53 (Hitler's own number was seven). Schreck was also one of the first members of the brownshirted SA Stormtroopers, and helped found the *Stosstrupp* Hitler/Adolf Hitler Patrol, the forerunner of the later SS.

Indeed, at his 1936 funeral RFSS Himmler called him "The first SS man," but author Charles Hamilton claims that he was actually SS Man #5. The Shock Troop Adolf Hitler (or Adolf Hitler Patrol) was replaced in 1925 when Schreck founded the *Schutzkommando*, the direct forerunner of the SS.

Added Hamilton in 1984, "Schreck is remembered with fondness by the surviving members of Hitler's inner circle. A well-liked man, he was apparently on very good terms with

Hitler, who was distraught when he died. From 1925-36 he was never very far from Hitler's side. His last position, succeeding Emil Maurice, was that of Hitler's personal chauffeur."

An insomniac, Hitler used to wake Schreck and his other chauffeurs and adjutants for long drives on country roads when he couldn't sleep. The original members of the 1925-26 *Schutzkommando*/Security Squad were Schreck, Julius Schaub, Hansgeorg Maurer, Emil Maurice, and Edmund Schneider.

Hitler never forgot chauffeur Schreck, and on the evening of January 24-25, 1942—six years after his early death at age 37—recalled his old friend and compared him and his successor Erich Kempka during a monologue at *FHQ Ft. Wolf* at Rastenburg, in East Prussia, following the German defeat at the Battle of Moscow.

"My life is in the hands of a few individuals: my driver, my orderlies, perhaps also a cook...Kempka's been in my service nine years now, and I've nothing but praise for him. His predecessor—Schreck!—was a companion of the years of struggle. When things went badly around us, the frontline soldier awoke in him! In such situations, Kempka would perhaps have fainted, but he drives with extraordinary prudence—always excepting when he's suffering from unrequited love, and that I notice at once.

"I've always insisted with my drivers—Maurice, Schreck, and Kempka—that the speed at which they drive should allow them to pull up in time in any circumstances. If one of my drivers killed a child, and excused himself by saying that he'd sounded his horn, I'd tell him: 'A child has no judgment; it's for *you* to think!'"

After Hitler became Reich Chancellor on January 30, 1933, driver Schreck was then authorized to protect the *Führer* with armed force if necessary during their joint journeys by car—not to mention himself.

When Hitler reportedly tried to shoot himself over the suicide of his niece and possible lover Geli Raubal in September 1931, allegedly it was Schreck (and Hess) who pulled the pistol from his hand, thus saving the *Führer's* life for his later rendezvous with the history of the Second World War.

In January 1942 Hitler recalled, "Kempka is calm personified. Besides, I'm accustomed to chatting with him. Eickenburg drives well, but I'd have to train him. He drives well mechanically, but he hasn't the initiative. I've done more than 2 ½ million kilometers by car, without the slightest accident (sic). When I drove with drivers for whose training I was not responsible, it was a matter of luck that nothing happened!" he told his intimates at table at *FHQ* during the war.

"I find it unpleasant when a car splashes mud on people lined up on the edge of a road, especially when they're people in their Sunday clothes. If my car passes a cyclist, I don't allow my driver to keep up the same speed, except when the wind immediately scatters the dust that we raise. When the rear tires shriek, that's a sign that the driver has taken a bend badly. It's a rule that one should only accelerate only in the bend, never before. The more our drivers succeed—on the whole—in driving well (although not exactly in the manner that suits me), the more our ruling class drives miserably! Of course, I've not invented the theory of driving, but I can learn from other people's experiences. Adolf Müller took me once into his car. Thanks to him, I learned more in a few hours than during the years that had gone before."

On February 10, 1942, Hitler said—wistfully—"When one has been driven for years by the same men, one no longer sees them as drivers, but as Party comrades." Schreck was just as anti-Jewish as Hitler. Once, as a train full of Nazis was stopped at a station in Nürnberg in 1933, Jews in a parked train opposite began jeering at the Nazis. Schreck "Leapt into the midst of them and started laying about him."

On August 13, 1932—expecting to be given the post of Chancellor—Hitler met with Reich President Paul von Hindenburg, but was only offered the second post in the government, that of Vice Chancellor, and turned it down. The Gregor Strasser socialist wing of the Nazi Party criticized him for this.

Later, Schreck drove Hitler south to Berchtesgaden, to plan his next moves. As they drove along Hitler muttered to himself, "We shall see. Perhaps it is better so. I would rather besiege a fortress than be a prisoner of it. Later on, we shall say that everything had to happen this way."

In January 1942 Hitler recalled that, "Schreck was as strong as a buffalo, and cold-bloodedly fearless."

Stated noted SS authority Bruce Quarrie, "Schreck, who became Hitler's chauffeur after his release from Landsberg prison, formulated the ground rules for admission into the SS, which were later to be polished and refined by Himmler." Schreck and his successor as head of the SS— Josef Berchtold—were unable to keep pace with the SA, however, and on January 6, 1929, this led to the appointment by Hitler of Heinrich Himmler as RFSS, which delighted the SA because they felt that they could control the weak-looking "Heini," but he surprised them all in 1934 with the Blood Purge.

Quarrie called Schreck, "A man virtually unrecognized in the history books, but one who had an unparalleled effect on the SS' eventual character and motivation." Neither Hitler nor the Nazi Party ever forgot his true role in their history, as most writers have done since 1936. Hopefully, this account—and my earlier works—will help put his real role back into true perspective at last.

Allegedly, former British Prime Minister Margaret Thatcher gave her late chauffeur a funeral while she was still in office. If not—or even if so—SS man Julius Schreck may be the only chauffeur in history to receive a formal State Funeral, on May 16, 1936.

Schreck's name was also commemorated on a Nazi Party "Germany Awake" standard, a high honor that no other *Führer* chauffeur ever achieved. German author Wulf Schwarzwaller claimed that Schreck joined the Nazi Party in 1921 and, "Occasionally, because of the resemblance, acted as Hitler's double."

In his 1937 book *I Knew Hitler* German author Kurt G.W. Ludecke wrote, "Beside him (Hitler), feet planted firmly on the ground, stood the Führer's ever-ready, ever-faithful dummy, his sturdy, strong-faced driver, Julius Schreck. This blunt Bavarian was to me the most sympathique and sincere person on Hitler's staff...It was rumored that he had been the victim of a murderous attack intended for Hitler, whom he resembled at a distance, except that his hair was black and his eyes dark."

The *Führer's* hair was brown and his eyes bright blue. In German, Schreck's name translates as "terror or fright," a suitable name for a man who was such a ferocious fighter against Hitler's political enemies.

During the war Hitler recalled, fondly, "What fun we had teasing the big American cars! We kept right behind them until they tried to lose us. Those Americans are junk compared to a Mercedes! Their motor couldn't take it. After awhile it would overheat, and they'd have to pull over to the side of the road, looking glum. Served them right!"

Recalled Hitler's architect, Albert Speer, in his 1970 work *Inside the Third Reich: Memoirs*, "During these stormy scenes of homage by the populace" (on their drives) which certainly affected me as well, there was one person in our car who refused to be carried away: Hitler's chauffeur of many years, Schreck.

"I heard some of his mutterings: 'Folks are dissatisfied because...Party people swell-headed...proud, forget where they come from...' After his early death, an oil painting of Schreck hung in Hitler's private office at Obersalzberg side by side with one of Hitler's mother—there was none of his father."

Now we turn to Lothar Machtan's view of the Schreck saga: "...Hitler's relations with Hess, Schreck, and Maurice really were like that: sustained by an awareness of mutual affection and loyalty. These 'employer-employee relationships' could not on any account be allowed to look like homosexual partnerships, however. This was probably why, during the post-Landsberg years, women suddenly appeared in Hitler's life, his public life included....

"Hitler's right-hand man: Julius Schreck. The scene in the New Cemetery at Grafeling, near München, on May 19, 1936, resembled a State occasion. The Nazi elite had turned out, almost to a man, to pay their last respects to Hitler's chauffeur, Julius Schreck. No chauffeur can ever have been escorted to the grave with greater ceremony, but Schreck was more than just a faithful retainer.

"Hitler personally laid the first wreath, which was dedicated to 'my faithful old fellow fighter and beloved comrade.' Even when he arrived, noted a reporter from the *People's Observor*, his face reflected, 'All the emotion of a man who had lost his comrade, his right-hand man in a long, hard life of struggle.'"

"Hitler was profoundly distressed by the death of this 'right-hand man'—so distressed that he had to leave the cemetery after Heinrich Himmler's brief eulogy. Hitler himself spoke no farewell words during the ceremony, nor did he speak much in general at the time. He was not seen again in public until May 30th. The commemorative addresses and eulogies delivered by his closest associates indicated what he was either incapable of saying or reluctant to show, namely, how hard hit he had been by the loss of this 'tough but warm-hearted old warhorse.'"

"Schreck's 'love' for the Führer had been boundless,' wrote Rudolf Hess. Similarly his 'indefatigable solicitude for the Führer,' whose 'supreme trust' he had always enjoyed. Himmler, too, alluded in his graveside address to Schreck's knack of 'reading the Führer's every wish and thought in his eyes, and fulfilling them.'

"Julius Schreck was only in his late thirties (37) when he unexpectedly died of an infection. He had made Vize-Feldwebel (roughly staff sergeant) in World War I, and had joined the Epp Free Corps in May 1919. In the spring of 1923, he and Josef Berchtold jointly founded the Stosstrupp Hitler/Hitler Assault Squad. Schreck's police record for this period lists various offenses ranging from fraud, breaches of the peace, and the use of offensive language, to grievous bodily harm.

"When the November 1923 *Putsch* failed, he fled to Austria [as did Göring], but was arrested at the frontier early in 1924 and received a suspended sentence of 15 months' detention. In 1925, the Stabswache/Headquarters Guard was formed under his command, and he was its first commander when it was renamed the Schutzstaffel/SS. In April 1926, however, when Berchtold...returned from exile in Austria, Schreck was relieved of his command in short order. The SS chiefs were of the opinion that 'Schreck is not equipped with the requisite talent for leadership and organization, nor does he possess a reputation which guarantees that the SS will become an elite formation of the Movement.'

"This setback did not deter Hitler from employing Schreck as his chauffeur, in other words, Maurice's successor, two years later. Although Schreck had occasionally driven the Party leader before that, he was at his service around the clock from 1928 on, for private trips as well as political engagements.

"When Hitler became better known—not least because of the countless political tours he undertook—'Schreck of the Highroad' also acquired a certain notoriety. 'He always knew at once whether to bring his physical strength, or his cunning, or his driving into play,' wrote Schaub, thereby intimating that Schreck was far more to Hitler than a willing chauffeur.

"His skillful piloting of Hitler's speedy, eye-catching Mercedes limousine suited his boss's taste for effective publicity. Not only must Hitler have found their fast and frequent trips by car extremely pleasurable, but they undoubtedly helped to enhance his image, and symbolized the advent of a dynamic new era.

"Even members of the Nazi inner circle turned to Hitler's constant companion when they wanted to gain swift, direct access to the Führer, or inform him of something in confidence. Albert Speer recalled that Schreck rather impudently took advantage of his position to make 'caustic remarks to Hitler about the fawning courtiers who surrounded him. He was the only person who was allowed such liberties.'

"Rumors circulated after his death that he had fallen prey to an attempt on Hitler's life, the assassins having erred in their aim because the two men looked so much alike. They did, in fact, display strong outward similarities. Although Schreck was somewhat more thickset and fuller in the face than Hitler, they resembled each other in height and hair coloring. Like his boss, Schreck parted his hair on the right and—the most conspicuous feature of all—sported the same clipped mustache.

"The two men had developed an unceremonious relationship on their innumerable trips across the length and breadth of Germany. Hitler would lovingly 'feed' his chauffeur en route 'by passing him pieces of bread'—a trivial gesture, but highly indicative of their informal manner with each other. Moreover, far from all their joint tours were undertaken because of political commitments. They would frequently set off into the blue just 'to enjoy the German countryside away from the main roads.'

"Excursions of that kind had been simpler when Hitler was less well known, Schreck wrote in 1935. 'Many a time one could stay the night at some inn, or have a meal without being recognized.' Few details of these trips are on record, of course, but at least one episode from 1931 is documented. Hitler had announced his intention of spending Christmas at Haus Wahnfried in Bayreuth, but the Wagners awaited his arrival in vain. A phone call to München elicited that Hitler and Schreck had, indeed, set off, but it was not until a few days later that Hitler informed his friend Winifred Wagner that he had preferred to be alone, and made an excursion into the countryside.

"Hitler and Schreck had stopped off at Bad Berneck, a health resort some 20 kilometers from Bayreuth, and spent the holiday at the Hotel Bube, a favorite of Hitler's entourage ever since 1923. They were the only guests.

"Julius Schreck had married in 1920. Officially, he and his wife Maria lived in München with his mother, Magda Schreck, until the 1930s. He then moved to Grafeling, leaving his wife behind with his mother, but without divorcing her. A few weeks after his death, Magda and Maria Schreck approached Hitler for money.... Maria's unmistakable allusion to her peculiar marital circumstances at once bore fruit: Hitler decreed that his late chauffeur's salary should, until further notice, be paid to his mother and his wife in equal shares."

Regarding the Hotel Bube—possibly a gay haunt—Machtan states that "The daughter of the owner of the hotel, Frau Jobst...saw Hitler three or four times a year prior to 1933, not only alone, but in the company of men, his close friend Julius Schreck in particular. There were never any women around."

Erich Kempka, 1910-75

As I wrote in *Apex of Glory* in 2006, "Schreck died on May 16, 1936, from cerebrospinal meningitis, leaving the position of chauffeur to Hitler open. SS Officer Erich Kempka would take over this position.

"During a discussion in 1942, Hitler compared Kempka with Schreck: 'If I need to know the time, I can rely on the clock on the car instrument panel. All the instruments are in perfect working order. I've never had a more conscientious driver! In utterly critical situations, he wouldn't have the same calmness as Schreck. He's entirely wrapped up in his driving. When I had Schreck beside me, it was the old wartime comrade at the wheel.'

"On another occasion, Hitler said, 'Kempka impeccably manages the collection of cars for which he's responsible. When I ask him—in September—if he has his stock of oil for the winter and his snow chains, I know he's ready equipped.'

"Kempka outlined in his postwar biography—*I Burned Hitler*—(the title being published against the wishes of Kempka), as Chief of the Motor Vehicle Division within the Reich Chancellery, he was responsible for approximately 400 men (drivers, mechanics, other staff) and 120 vehicles. Kempka remained with Hitler until the end, only leaving the besieged Reich Chancellery after Hitler was dead," on April 30, 1945.

Basically, Kempka was the sole *Führer* chauffeur from the time of Schreck's death in 1936 until Hitler's suicide. According to author Peter Hoffmann in *Hitler's Personal Security*, by January 1939 a rigid strata of those officials to be told in advance of a *Führer* car trip had already been worked out for wartime.

After the war Kempka was one of the main German witnesses testifying that Martin Bormann had been killed in Berlin on May 1, 1945, by a tank explosion. Kempka's official title was Chief of the *Führer's* and Reich Chancellor's Fleet of Cars according to Peter Hoffmann, who also asserted that 50 was the mandatory retirement age for Hitler's drivers.

Kempka was seized at Berchtesgaden by the American Army in May 1945, and testified on the witness stand at Nürnberg on July 4, 1946, where he was asked, "In what capacity were you employed near Hitler during the war?" Kempka answered, "During the war, I worked for Adolf Hitler as his personal driver." Thus, he entered history as a personal witness to the deaths of the two Hitlers—Adolf and Eva—the Gœbbels family, and his former boss, Martin Bormann.

Before joining Hitler's own staff as one of his SS bodyguards, Kempka had been Josef Terboven's driver, but transferred to the *Führer's* service on March 1, 1932, and thus had been with Hitler for more than four years by the time of Schreck's death in May 1936. Born September 16, 1910, Kempka was only 21 when he came to Hitler as both a member of the Nazi Party and the SS, and still only 34 years old 13 years later at "The Chief's" death in 1945.

Born a Rhinelander, Kempka was the son of a miner, and one of nine brothers and sisters. He left school at age 14 to become a mechanic and apprentice electrician. By 1945 his hatred of Martin Bormann—his boss under Hitler—was well developed, as he noted after the war: "Those of us who had to work for long years in close proximity to this diabolical personality hated him."

Earlier, before his own rise to power, Bormann had sought to ingratiate himself with the man he would one day supervise, "with a catlike, overbearing friendliness," Kempka recalled, adding, "In those days, he was a very small man in the organization...He had an extraordinary ability to give his equals the impression that he was a good fellow, and to make himself popular with his superiors," first Hess, and then Hitler.

With his underlings, however, he was another man altogether, Kempka asserted. "He was brutal in the extreme," he noted in his 1952 memoirs. "If there was anything good at all about him, it must've been his enormous capacity for work. One cannot deny that he worked day and night, almost without pause."

Kempka later recalled an incident when he, Hitler, and Martin Bormann stood on the terrace of The Beghof admiring a view that the *Führer* lamented was broken only by an old peasant's house. One day later, after driving to Münich and back to Berchtesgaden, they noticed that Bormann had had the house removed to please Hitler, and that in its place was a meadow upon which cows grazed, so determined was Bormann to burrow into the *Führer's* favor; he succeeded.

By 1945, as Berlin was besieged by the Red Army, there were 22 Mercedes cars and half-tracked vehicles in the Reich Chancellery Garage for which Kempka was then responsible. In a June 18, 1949, diary entry made while a convict at Spandau Prison outside Berlin, Speer recalled when the SS would admit thousands of Germans onto The Berghof property five abreast to meet their *Führer* in person: "Hitler would point out one child or another to his chauffeur, Kempka, and an SS man would then lift the child above the crowd. Then the inevitable group picture would be taken."

Of his chauffeurs and RSD/SS bodyguards, Hitler vowed that he would never willingly part with any of them, since they had risked their lives for him. Kempka survived his Nazi master and was part of the breakout from the embattled Reich Chancellery in Berlin on May 1, 1945. Noted SS aide Otto Günsche of this escape, "Some people decided to wear civilian clothes—Axmann, Naumann, and Kempka, for example—but others, like myself, kept their uniforms."

Because Kempka today is far better known than his predecessor Schreck—mainly due to his appearance in all of the "Hitler's last days" books, articles, television shows, and movies—many authors have mistakenly called him "Hitler's favorite driver," but the current writer believes that accolade more properly belongs to Schreck instead.

German author Hans-Otto Meissner—son of Old Reich Chancellery/NewRC State Secretary Dr. Otto Meissner—met Kempka in an Allied POW camp in late 1947: "I came to know Kempka, a quiet, unassuming, extremely reserved man." The camp was Ludwigsburg Ossweil. Author Meissner reported in his biography of Magda Göbbels, *The First Lady of the Third Reich*, that Kempka begged her to escape the Berlin Bunker in 1945 using a trio of armored cars that he had under his charge.

Magda hesitated in her previous resolve to kill both herself and her six children. This conversation was overheard by Dr. Josef Gœbbels, who said that his wife was free to escape, but that he would stay and die with the *Führer*. Recalled Kempka to Meissner, Magda immediately rejoined thus: "That goes for me, too! The children and I stay here, thank you very much all the same, Herr Kempka!"

Meissner also reported in the same work that, in 1945 in the Bunker, Kempka performed a wedding ceremony *after* that of the two Hitlers, with him acting as the minister for one of his own subordinate officers. "The bride—who'd been severely wounded—lay on a stretcher, and was given pain-killing drugs during the ceremony." It is not known if the couple survived, however.

Noted Hitler's final personal secretary, Traudl Humps Junge, "The only fear that Hitler had about driving through big crowds was that a child might fall under the wheels of his car." None ever did, though, at least as far as is known. After the war she recalled a funny story, in Hitler's own words: "Before the war, I used to go on long car journeys across the country with my Party comrades. Once...when my line of cars was recognized, a huge number of cars joined the procession, and it was impossible to escape for a moment alone in the woods along the roadside, so we kept going for hours without stopping... Behind me, Brückner and Schaub were suffering agonies, their teeth clenched. I had to stand there saluting and smiling for hours."

In his book *10 Days to Die*, American author Judge Michael A. Musmanno reported that Hitler did not approve of the marriage of Kempka to his wife Maja so the driver divorced her, but lived with her secretly until after Hitler's death so as to avoid being sent to the Russian Front as a punishment for ignoring the *Führer's* wishes. Hitler liked docile women, not those with the haughty air possessed by Maja Kempka. "A great man should marry a stupid woman!" Hitler proclaimed, often in the presence of his mistress and later wife, Eva Braun Hitler. It also developed later that Maja Kempka was a prosititute.

Ike and His Chauffeur/Lover, Kay Summersby

Hitler wasn't the only one! World War II Allied Supreme Commander in Europe Gen. Dwight D. Eisenhower (1890-1969) allegedly made his British female driver, Kay Summersby (1908-75), both his lover and a commissioned captain in the United States Army, as detailed in her 1976 book *Past Forgetting: My Love Affair with Dwight D. Eisenhower*.

The former member of the British Motor Transport Corps—in which the current Queen Elizabeth II also served during the Second World War—drove Ike's standard U.S. Army Packard staff car. Like Hitler, the general preferred to ride in front with his driver, not in the passenger section behind.

After the war Ike dumped Kay, returned home to live with his wife Mamie in the U.S., and went on to become President of Columbia University in New York, and later also President of the United States during 1953-61. He died in 1969.

The Packard was a five-passenger medium sedan of which the U.S. military had 487 built during 1940-43, and the British had 56 as well. Marshal Mannerheim of Finland also had a V12 Packard. Ike's car registration number was R-126144.

Cars and Drivers During the *Kampfzeit*/Time of Struggle, 1919-33

The Nazis called the time before they took office on January 30, 1933, as the *Kampfzeit*, or The Time of Struggle. Recalled one observer of Hitler's motorcades then, "The crowds and the joy were just endless. You didn't actually get an impression of someone driving past. There were huge crowds with ladders and stools, and I don't know what! Some of them had been standing there for an hour already," according to a German author in the work *Did You Ever See Hitler?*

Wrote one auto mechanic, "When I shook his hand I thought, 'You can't obey every order he gives you if you want to survive!'" One lady later recalled this somewhat embarrassing incident in Berlin, when she saw Hitler's car go by: 'There was a coffee house with a lamp shop nearby...I had to go to the toilet, and in the toilet, I opened the window a little so that I could look out while sitting down. Suddenly, Hitler drives past outside, standing in his car, and looks directly into the toilet, and sees me sitting there with a naked behind. Man, did I ever shut that window!'"

Noted one physician in 1973, "We marched past in rows of 12 with the Hitler Youth, feeling really elated. He stood in his car, in his typical pose, that fascinated us somehow. Everyone felt somehow that Hitler was looking at him."

Recalled another German observer, "Suddenly, people said, 'The Führer is coming!' and everyone pushed forward so that they could see him, and there came an open car—a Mercedes, not that I'm sure what kind of car it was—and Hermann Göring was inside it, and the Minister of the Interior Frick" (after 1933). Hitler stood and waved, and for us it was a feeling of bliss."

Eva Braun Hitler biographer Glenn Infield stated that Hitler acquired his first fleet of Mercedes cars in 1929, most likely with the help of Münich dealer Jakob Werlin.

Noted Schreck himself in an article published in 1936 before his death, "The children were usually the first to recognize him. The moment they realized it was the Führer who was passing through their village, they would race to the cars in hopes that they might give him flowers or shake his hand. The children would fight through the crowds to be near him, and the Führer often told his driver to stop in order that he could converse with the children and give them autographs."

After the double loss of the 1932 German Presidential elections to incumbent Field Marshal Paul von Hindenburg, however, the Nazi Party treasury was bare, and it looked as if the Party might fall apart altogether. Hitler's fortunes—on the very eve of his being appointed Reich Chancellor by the man who'd just twice defeated him!—were at their lowest ebb since the failed Beer Hall *Putsch* almost a decade earlier.

Even the *Chauffeureska* intimates grew dejected and rude, as recounted by Schwarzwäller in *The Unknown Hitler*: "A downcast Hitler sat in his suite at the Kaiserhof/ Imperial Hotel in Berlin, waiting for his soup. 'Where is it?' he demanded, calling out to the hallway where his bodyguards and chauffeurs were loitering. 'He wants his soup,' one of them said, followed by laughter from the others. 'Go get him his soup!' another one said, again followed by laughter. No one made a move to get his soup, the dissension in the ranks was so great that it had now affected the chauffeurs.

"Rudolf Hess rose from the table beside Hitler and walked into the hallway, his face chalk-white and his lips pressed together in anger. He hissed a few words, and one of the chauffeurs sullenly went to find the soup."

Many in the Party had sharply criticized the leader of a workers' party—Hitler of the Nazis—for having an expensive, luxury automobile during the height of the Depression, but he defended having the car with the reasoning that it would make the Party seem more successful to the average person than it actually was. It did.

The Nazis did well in the 1928 *Reichstag*/Parliamentary national elections, and on October 11, 1931, participated in the nationalist Harzburg Front with other right wing organizations, a first time gathering of all of the various groups. Hitler dominated it.

On August 13, 1932, President von Hindenburg had refused to name Hitler as Reich Chancellor with the same type of power that Benito Mussolini had gained in Savoyard Italy, in October 1922, a decade earlier. After running against and losing to von Hindenburg twice in 1932, it appeared that Hitler might never come to office. Sullenly he snapped, "I am 45. He is 82. I can wait."

Recalled Schreck of some of his dangerous journeys a decade afterward, "During the years of his political struggle, the Führer's motor trips led to potentially dangerous situations. No amount of danger would prevent Hitler from making his scheduled speeches, and often he drove through Bolshevik demonstrations. On more than one occasion, the car was surrounded by thousands of misled comrades, but the Leader remained calm, even when citizens with raised fists were glaring menacingly at him."

Indeed, Albert Speer was present during one of these—in July 1932— as he recalled in his 1970 work *Inside the Third Reich: Memoirs*: "The cars came. I took my passenger into my rattling roadster and drove at top speed a few minutes ahead of Hitler's motorcade. In Brandenburg (Berlin), the sidewalks close to the stadium were occupied by Social Democrats and Communists. With my passenger wearing the Party uniform, the temper of the crowd grew ugly.

"When Hitler with his entourage arrived a few minutes later, the demonstrators overflowed into the street. Hitler's car had to force its way through at a snail's pace.

"Hitler stood erect beside the driver. At that time, I felt respect for his courage, and still do."

In 1936 Schreck would write, "There have been times when mothers brought their children to the Führer's car, holding Germany's future in their arms. One such mother turned to her child and remarked, 'You belong to him.'"

President Paul von Hindenburg appointed Adolf Hitler Chancellor of the German Reich on January 30, 1933, and thus the Third Reich was born.

Here is the official Nazi Party eulogy for Schreck, as delivered by Rudolf Hess at the funeral and printed later that same year in the Heinrich Hoffmann picture book *Adolf Hitler: Scenes From the Life of the Führer*:

"The National Socialistic movement today says goodbye to Julius Schreck, one of the oldest and dearest followers. He was one of the best, and he will be irreplaceable. He was modest, and wanted nothing for himself, yet he gave everything for Germany and Adolf Hitler.

"When he was called to fight, he fought with loyalty and bravery. When called upon to serve in time of peace, he did so to the best of his ability. His admiration and love for Hitler was endless. He carefully protected our Leader from harm, and he was always reliable to the fullest degree. Julius Schreck's judgment of people was always correct.

"He displayed his likes and dislikes, and he was considered a rough man with a warm heart. He was feared by his enemies, loved by his friends, and admired as a father-like friend by his subordinates. Our Führer placed his highest confidence in this man. The Movement lowers the flags for the last greeting to Julius Schreck.

"It is the Movement's desire that his ways will become an example to all German citizens."

No wonder that people sometimes mistook chauffeur Schreck for his passenger, Hitler! Here the former follows his *Führer* at left in a pre-1930 arrival at a Nazi meeting. In 1942 Hitler reminisced, "I went to the Benz works, and thus made Werlin's acquaintance. I told him that I wanted to buy a 16hp car. 'You'll decide for yourself in the end,' he said. 'I'd advise you to try a 10hp to begin with, to get your hand in. It does only 80 km an hour, but it's better to arrive at your destination at 80, than to smash yourself up at 110'. These were so many dagger thrusts at my pride!" Hitler later remembered. (HHA.)

Here *Führer* SS chauffeur Julius Schreck is being lionized on film at the September 1934 Nazi Party Congress at Nürnberg for Leni Riefenstahl's 1935-released documentary film "Triumph of the Will." One account states that Schreck was killed in a May 1936 auto accident in which Hitler wasn't involved. (HHA.)

At the November 1934 annual observation of the 1923 Beer Hall *Putsch*, Hitler (left, center) appears with his former and estranged chauffeur, Emil Maurice (center, dark trousers), followed by Münich Hitler bodyguard and horse-trader/bouncer Christian Weber, with Rudolf Hess seen just behind him in the distance. (HHA.)

At a Nazi Party meeting at Berlin's Hotel Kaiserhof in 1932, from left to right: Hess, Schreck, Schaub, unknown man, Bernhard Rust, and Hitler (hand on chin). (HHA.)

Chauffeur Schreck poses beside Hitler's 770K Grosser in the Old Reich Chancellery garage. Just under his left hand rests a special heating device to defrost the windshield. Note, too, the radiator, lamps, horns, and pennants, all under the logo of the three-pointed star. (HHA.)

Driver (left) and patron (second from right) inspect a Grosser at one of the prewar Berlin auto shows. At far right is Reich Photo Reporter Prof. Heinrich Hoffmann. (HHA.)

A 1933 road trip with, from left to righ: Hitler, Schreck (wearing leather motoring cap), unknown man, and Jakob Werlin. Recalled Hitler on February 10, 1942, "I've had some queer drivers in my time! Göring made a point of always driving on the left-hand side of the road! In moments of danger, he used to blow his horn. His confidence was unfailing, but it was of a somewhat mystic nature. Killinger was also an ace at the wheel! Once I saw Bastian get down peacefully from his car, knock out some fools who'd jeered at him, take the wheel again, and move off in complete calm...." (HHA.)

Car passengers all, Hitler's adjutants assemble for a group portrait with Dr. Josef Gœbbels at the Old German Reich Chancellery in Berlin in 1935. From left to right: SA Gen. Wilhelm Brückner; SS Julius Schreck; Reich Press Chief Dr. Otto Dietrich, also in SS black; Dr. Gœbbels; SSLAH chief Gen. Josef Sepp/Joe Dietrich; Hitler pilot Hans Baur; and SS Escort Physician Dr. Karl Brandt. Baur survived them all, dying at age 98 in 1993, after a decade of imprisonment in the USSR to boot! (HHA.)

"The *Chauffeureska*," from left to right: bodyguard Ulrich Graf, Rudolf Hess, Julius Schaub, Hitler, Schreck, and Christian Weber (back to camera.) The men are wearing the old style coffee can SS kepis that preceded the later soft caps. (HHA.)

Imperturbable, *Oberführer*/Senior Colonel SS chauffeur Julius Schreck sits at the wheel of Hitler's 770K Grosser. (HHA.)

Chauffeur Schreck drives his *Führer* into a crowd of pro-Nazi, enthusiastic supporters in an open tourer. Hitler rises to accept the accolades, while Wilhelm Frick gives a casual Nazi salute from the rear seat. Note the tread on the spare tire mounted on the side of the car. (HHA.)

Passenger and driver, with Schreck wearing the collar tabs of an SS brigadier general. (HHA.)

Hitler steps into his Mercedes, as SS bodyguard Karl Wilhelm Krause holds the door open and driver Julius Schreck looks back over his shoulder. The tall man standing on the landing above Hitler is Dr. Richard Schulze, a physician who treated his dislocated shoulder that was suffered on November 9, 1923, when Hitler fell—or was dragged—to the street as Münich police fired on the Nazi marchers attempting to seize power during the Beer Hall *Putsch*. At left, carrying his cap in his left hand is Alfred Rosenberg, the Nazi Party theorist whom Hitler planned to put in charge of conquered Soviet territory had World War II ended in a German victory. Instead, Rosenberg was hanged by the Allies as a war criminal at Nürnberg on October 16, 1946. In this picture, also note the reflection on the highly polished car door of the street cobblestones, as well as the engine visible through the side louvers on the hood, and Hitler's personal *Führer* Standard on the right front fender. (HHA.)

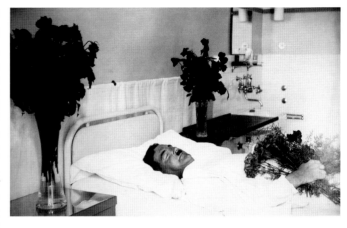

The death of a chauffeur: Julius Schreck, May 16, 1936. He was one of the first of Hitler's close comrades from the *Kampfzeit* Era to pass away, and the *Führer* took the loss hard. Here, the dead driver lies in his hospital bed, a bouquet of flowers in his right hand. There are two published versions of his early death at only 37. In the 1976 biography *Adolf Hitler*, American author John Toland (whom I met in Washington, DC, that same year at the National Archives) wrote, "It was a particularly trying time for Hitler. His chauffeur Schreck had recently been killed in a crash, and he himself was having trouble sleeping." The scar on the right side of Schreck's nose in this photo seems to bear this out, but another account disputes this. In his excellent, detailed 1984 work *Leaders and Personalities of the Third Reich* author Charles Hamilton stated that "He died of cerebrospinal meningitis on May 16, 1936, and was given a State Funeral." A doctor whom I consulted stated that the illness could've resulted *from* the crash, causing death, so maybe *both* accounts are correct. (HHA.)

Hitler and Schreck on Heroes' Memorial Day March 1935 in Berlin, with the *Führer's* naval and military aides in the rear. Note also that the windshield is in the down position. (HHA.)

The enduring image: Hitler saluting, and stolid, solid Schreck at the wheel outside the Hotel Excelsior, 1935. (HHA.)

The State Funeral for chauffeur Julius Schreck at Grafeling, May 16, 1936, as the crestfallen *Führer* (center) pauses in silence after having placed his wreath on the gravesite at right. Virtually the entire Nazi Party top strata leadership corps turned out for the ceremony, as seen here, from left to right: an unknown SS man; Wilhelm Frick; Martin Bormann; two unknown officials; Julius Streicher; Julius Schaub; Hess; Gœbbels; SA Chief of Staff Viktor Lütze; Hitler; Hermann Göring; Paul "Pilli" Körner (a Göring aide); Max Amann, the Nazi publisher; Labor Front leader Dr. Robert Ley; unknown man; Dr. Otto Dietrich; Dr. Walter Darré; NSKK chief Adolf Hühnlein; RFSS Himmler; two unknown men; Maj. Walther Buch; an unknown SS man; and Sepp Dietrich. (HHA.)

Maj. Kempka started driving Hitler periodically in 1932, and then exclusively after 1936 for the last nine years of their joint car careers, and for virtually *all* of World War II. Here is their enduring image together, driver and patron. (HHA.)

Above, left: The *Führer's* final and most famous chauffeur, SS officer Erich Kempka, 1935. As Hitler recalled in 1942, "In former times, I used to read regularly the publications devoted to the motor car, but I no longer have the time. Nevertheless, I continue to be interested in all new advances made in that field. I talk about them with Kempka. He's a man who knows all the motorcars in the world! It's a pleasure to see—since it's his job to bother about that—how well our motor park is kept." I first published this picture in 1999. It was also used in 2009 in The History Channel series *Hitler's Bodyguard.* (HHA.)

Above, right: The photo that was used with Kempka's newspaper obituary in 1975, when he died at age 65. Martin Bormann told Daimler-Benz management that no orders for Hitler's cars were valid unless they came in writing from him, Martin Bormann. Thus, it was Bormann's name—and not Hitler's (save one)—that appeared on all such car registries. (HHA.)

Maj. Kempka at the wheel, with Mussolini and Hitler in the passenger section during the State Visit of the *Duce/ Leader* to Nazi Germany in September 1937. (HHA.)

A smoking break for a trio of SS men at Castle Klessheim at Salzburg, Austria, during the war. From left to right, chauffeur Erich Kempka in wartime SS gray, RSD (Reich Security Service) chief Johann Rattenhuber, and Otto Gesche, head of the SS Begleitkommando. All three men survived the Second World War. (HHA.)

Gen. Dwight D. Eisenhower (left) and his wartime driver, U.S. Army Capt. Kay Summersby Morgan. (U.S. Army Signal Corps photo.)

SS Chauffeur Maj. Erich Kempka and Hitler in 1943 at *FHQ Ft. Wolf*, Rastenburg, East Prussia. (HHA.)

A scene from the August 1929 Nürnberg Party Day in what may have been one of the first of the *Führer's* Mercedes-Benz open tourers on what would be named Adolf Hitler Plaza in 1934. Here, a boyish-looking Hitler throws a bouquet of flowers to his marching men at left. Just under his arm can be seen (face hidden) Capt. Franz von Salomon und Pfeffer—SA Staff Chief from 1926-30—and standing at the right front door jamb, wearing SS kepis and looking into the camera lens, are bodyguard Ulrich Graf and Julius Schaub, both members of the early *Chauffeureska* (circle of chauffeurs). (HHA.)

There are only two *known* views of Hitler actually *wearing* an SA kepi. This is one of them, first published in 1976 by John Toland in *Adolf Hitler*. (HHA.)

This is the second known published view of Hitler wearing an SA cap, as published in the December 2005 issue of *Militaria Illustrated Magazine*, now defunct, unfortunately. Note the car tire tread. Covers have not been installed yet on the spare tires. Stated *MIM*, "The 1929 time frame seems logical in view of Hitler's kepi not bearing the first pattern NSDAP/SA M-1929 pointed wing eagle, a piece that was only introduced that year, as well as the use of the split window touring limo, a style that was discontinued in the early 1930s. This photo has been in the possession of an Army veteran for the last 60 years, an unexpected and a rare find," according to Manion's. (MIM.)

Hitler in motoring cap in 1923; not a Grosser. (HHA.)

Hitler Youth leaders Baldur von Schirach (front seat, leather motoring cap) and Artur Axmann (1913-96) (rear seat, hatless) in an open tourer in the early 1930s. When Schirach was named Gauleiter/Regional Leader of Vienna in 1940 by Hitler, Axmann succeeded him as HJ *Führer*. In the Army, Axmann served in the West in 1940, and on the Russian Front in 1941 until losing his right arm in combat. As Reich Youth Leader, Axmann led a battalion of boys in the Battle of Berlin in 1945 and saw the burning of the two Hitlers. The driver is unknown. (Eva Braun Hitler Albums, USNA, College Park, MD.)

Weary motorist Hitler stifles a yawn at Frankfurt during a campaign stop in the German Presidential Election of 1932, which he lost to the man who later appointed him Chancellor of the Reich, Field Marshal Paul von Hindenburg. At right, wearing motoring goggles and leather coat, is SA adjutant Wilhelm Brückner. In the background, with hair parted in the middle, is aide Ernst Putzi/Little Fellow Hanfstaengl, the man who coined the term "*chauffeureska*." Hitler wears a leather motoring cap and overcoat. (HHA.)

A roadside stop during the early 1930s, from left to right: unknown motorist, Hess in goggles, two unidentified men, and a jovial Hitler wearing leather motoring cap. Hitler studied road maps in order to avoid possible Communist ambushes along his route, and was, apparently, very good at it, too. (HHA.)

Hitler arriving at Nürnberg, 1929, with a relaxed Rudolf Hess in the back seat. The car is not a Grosser. Note the three SS men in the black coffee can style kepis outside the car at left. (HHA.)

Grosser Mercedes roadside reactions: Hitler shakes hands with an admirer before his appointment as Reich Chancellor during one of his *Kampfzeit* cross-country tours of the land he hoped one day to lead. (HHA.)

A joyous Hitler reacts with pleasure upon being lustily greeted by passing SA men in the rain. Note Hitler's Sam Browne belt. I've had this exceptional photo in my files for 40 years, and it is here published for the very first time anywhere. (Heinrich Hoffmann Albums, U.S. National Archives, College Park, MD.)

The *Führer* in his open tourer Mercedes in Münich in 1930 with a few of his *Alte Kampfer*/Old Fighters, original Nazi Party members from the early 1920s, the men who'd backed him from the start. Hitler gives a casual, backhand salute, while—outside the car—from left to right: Münich Gauleiter Adolf Wagner, Party finance chief Franz Xavier Schwarz, and Phillip Bouhler, Party Secretary General during 1925-34, who handled Hitler's personal affairs for him until the advent of the shadowy aide Martin Bormann that year. Noted Julius Schreck in 1936 of this period: "I was privileged to be a constant companion of the *Führer* on his motor trips, and I can recall a thousand pictures...Wherever the *Führer* went, he was greeted by throngs of children and adults who expressed their love for him, and their faith in his leadership." (HHA.)

Two unusual views of Hermann Göring inside the *Führer's* open tourer while Hitler (left) stands outside the car with Nazi leader Fritz Sauckel (1894-1946). Oddly, both Hitler and Göring seem to be giving the raised, clenched fist salute of the German Communist Party, and none of the trio look very happy! Sauckel—a Göring man—was Gauleiter of Thuringia during 1927-45, and was German foreign manpower tsar during 1942-45, for which he was hanged as a convicted war criminal at Nürnberg in place of Speer. A seaman in 1910, Sauckel was imprisoned by the French in 1914 when the First World War broke out, and remained interned for the next five years. As an engineering student in Germany, Sauckel joined the Nazis in 1923. Gœbbels called him "The dullest of the dull." (HHA.)

On January 30, 1933, Hitler left his Berlin Party headquarters at the Hotel Kaiserhof for his first Cabinet meeting at the Reich Chancellery after his historic appointment by President von Hindenburg. He is seen here entering his Mercedes Pullman Saloon car. Thus, the Nazi swastika was literally driven to power by the Daimler-Benz three-pointed star. The car was a Mercedes Nürburg, and not a Grosser. (HHA.)

A joyous Nazi crowd greets Hitler's car in the Wilhelmstrasse on Monday, January 30, 1933, held back by Berlin Regular Police, who today still wear the same style helmets. This is Hitler's own view of his moment of triumph, as seen from behind the windshield of his Mercedes-Benz Pullman Saloon car. The steering wheel is also seen at left. Noted American author William L. Shirer, in his 1960 seminal work *The Rise and Fall of the Third Reich*, "He drove the hundred yards to the Kaiserhof, and was soon with his old cronies, Gœbbels, Göring, Röhm, and the other Brownshirts who had helped him along the rocky, brawling path to power." Noted Gœbbels later, "He says nothing, and all of us say nothing, but his eyes are full of tears." Hitler had been appointed to office after 13 years of political struggle, a period in which he had held no State office, gone to jail for a failed revolt, run in and lost two Presidential elections back to back within a month, and fought and won two national *Reichstag* elections. In the words of Britain's great Jewish Prime Minister, Benjamin Disraeli, Hitler had climbed "To the top of the greasy pole." (HHA.)

3

The 770K Grosser Model

The Kaiser's 1941 Hearse

His Imperial Hohenzollern Majesty Kaiser Wilhelm II (1859-1941) may very well have been the only historic personage to have his normal touring car converted into his hearse at his death on June 4, 1941.

The car was a Grosser/Grand Mercedes 770K (with an M 07 naturally aspirated engine.) The line was produced during 1930-38, had a four-stroke Otto combustion principle and eight inline cylinders, with a front, longitudinal, vertical configuration. Its bore by stroke was 95 x 135 mm, it had a total displacement of 7655 cc (tax classification 7603 cc), a compression ratio of 4.7, and nine crankshaft bearings.

Its rated output was 150 hp at 2800 rpm, it had a single intake valve and one overhead exhaust, a sole lateral camshaft, spur gear camshaft drive, and a fuel system that consisted of a Mercedes-Benz triple-jet double carburetor. It was water cooled with a 32 l water pump, a pressure circulation 9 l oil lubrication system, and a 12 Volt electrical system, with a 75 ah battery and 225 W generator.

It also had an electrical starter that was at first 2.5 hp, and later 2.8 hp, with a double ignition (magneto and battery ignition), with two plugs per cylinder, and a rear mounted fuel tank of 120 liters capacity.

A total of 117 of this model were built. The prices were: chassis 29,000 Reich Marks (RM); six-seat tourer 39,000 RM; Pullman limousine: 38,000 RM; convertible C 41,500 RM; convertible B, D; and F 44,500 RM.

The model wheelbase was 3,750 mm; its front and rear tracks 1,500 mm; and it was 5,600 mm long and 1,840 mm wide, with a height of 1,830 mm. Its turning circle diameter was 14.1 m, the chassis weighed 1,950 kg, and its gross weight was 3,500 kg. Its curb weight was 2,700 kg.

It had a three-speed manual transmission gearing with additional overdrive with a central steering column shifting lever to engage the overdrive gear. It also boasted a dry, double-disc clutch with a change speed transmission type gear and 2, 3, and over-drive

As I wrote in 1999, "Hitler at the very apex of his glory, July 6, 1940, in IA-148461." According to author Aaron L. Johnson in his 2001 work *Hitler's Military Headquarters*, "Hitler's return to his capital after the brilliantly successful campaign in the West was a great personal triumph for him. The streets of Berlin between the railroad station and the Chancellery on the Wilhelmsplatz were packed with cheering Berliners. The streets were covered with flowers, and all of the church bells of Berlin rang." Note the headlamp covers with their nighttime driving slits. Notes Sutton, "It was not until the 1930s that bright electric lights were fitted as standard on most cars...and headlights...were included in the car's overall styling." (HHA.)

Synchromesh gears. Its gear ratios were 1: 2.73; 2: 1.52; 3 1.0; and S 0.71 or 0.76. Its final drive ratio was 4.50; 4.88; or 4.30, and its maximum speed was 150 km an hour. Fuel consumption was 29 liters.

A Car Fit for a *Führer*: The Super Mercedes

Hitler—both as rising politician and Führer and Reich Chancellor—was a devoted Mercedes-Benz customer during 1924-45, as well as His Majesty before him. Jakob Werlin sold him his first Mercedes, and also ordered a special 770K for his Führer's 50th birthday gala on April 20, 1939, a cabriolet D with four doors and seven seats: quite a birthday present! The normal model cost 46,000 RM, but his special version was priced at 47,500 RM. It had 18 mm thick armor plating, 40 mm thick bulletproof windows, explosion-proof, 20 chamber cellular tires, and side-mounted spare tires in the twin wings. Noted one source: "The car had become a political tool: cars for the masses was the byword."

Hitler's cars sat seven-eight passengers, had eight cylinders, a bore 0f 95 mm, stroke of 135 mm, cubic capacity of 7,655 ccm; 2,000 engine revolutions at 62 mph in fourth speed, a brake hp of 155/230 hp, a wheelbase of 12' 11 1.8"; a front track of 5'4", a rear track of 5'6"; its overall length was 20 feet, the overall height with body (without passengers) was 6'; the overall width with body was 6'10 ¾"; a ground clearance of 8'; a chassis weight of approximately 44 cwts; the weight of the complete car was approximately 68-72 cwts; the total reduction in top gear was 1:2.96; tires were 8.25-17; the turning circle was 55'; the maximum speed by the stop watch was approximately 107 mph; the Autobahn cruising speed was 90 mph; standard fuel consumption was 9 mpg; oil consumption was 900 mpg; the capacity of the fuel tank was 43 gallons, including a reserve of 4 ½ gallons; the climbing ability in 1st gear was 1 in 2 ½; climbing ability in 2nd gear was 1 in 3 ¾; climbing ability in 3rd gear was 1 in 5; climbing ability in 4th gear was 1 in 8; and the capacity of the battery was 75 amps hrs, as recorded in the 1930s Daimler-Benz sales brochure.

There were two generations of Grosser Mercedes cars: the W 07 manufactured between 1930-38, and the W 150 built during 1938-43, all with chromium-plated exhaust pipes on the right side of the engine.

The Grosser was probably the most famous model that the firm has ever built to date. Called the "Super Mercedes," its 1930s sale brochure read, "Equipped with the result of every achievement in up-to-date automobile technique, the Type Super Mercedes has reaped the benefit of the numerous experiences gained in international automobile racing events of the most grueling nature. So, for instance, the chassis frame—which consists of welded oval tubes, and with which the front wall is organically connected, resembles, constructionally that of the victorious Mercedes-Benz racing cars.

"The 'laterally stable parallel wheel axle with coil springs' has also been taken over from the racing car. The advantages of this type of axle are that all moments and forces are absorbed by special elements, thus preventing their transmission to chassis and body. A further advantage of this construction is that the lateral incline of the car body in bends is reduced to a minimum.

"The mode of operations of the entire springing system of this car gives a driving comfort unequalled by any other make. Particular care was devoted to achieving easy functioning of all operating organs and—to that end— the clutch is hydraulically operated.

The hydraulic brakes are Servo-assisted, and give the greatest possible braking effect with a minimum of physical effort.

"The powerful and elastic Straight Eight engine develops 155 BHP without—and 230 BHP with—the Supercharger engine. A noiseless five-speed geabox—2nd to 5th speed Synchromesh—is fitted with the same perfection also featured in the design and equipment of the coachwork models, in construction of which every conceivable wish of the buyer will be readily acceded to."

Noted author Griffith Borgeson in *The First Century*, "The engine was an immense pushrod straight eight, whose 95 x 135 bore and stroke...gave a displacement of 7,655 cc, from which the chassis' type nomenclature was derived. The crankshaft rode in nine main bearings, and dual ignition was provided, as in the S series by both battery and magneto. The maximum of 150 hp was developed at a mere 2000 rpm by this fully-balanced and silk-smooth power plant."

He wrote of the power plant, "An additional 50 BHP became available at the same peak revs (2000 rpm) with the installation of the optional Supercharger. Torque was tremendous. It was fed to a synchronized transmission, which also had three speeds plus overdrive, then by torque tube to a solid rear axle....

"The brakes were mechanical, with vacuum assist, and chassis lubrication was automatic. The complete car had much in common with the current 16-cylinder Cadillac; both had a wheelbase of 148" and an all-up weight of around 6,000 pounds. Unblown, a typical 770 would match the big Cad's 93 mph; with Supercharger engaged, about 100 mph was attainable. It is oddly appropriate that the recommended weight of the 770 was 3500 kg—exactly 7700 pounds....

"Most of the select output remained in Germany, in the service of top government officials. Only 88 of these most impressive of ceremonial coaches were produced."

Indeed, according to Leo Levine in 1986, "The label of parade car builder to the Nazi Party—though the company had no choice in the matter—has been hard to shake." I contradict this; I believe that the company had every choice to make, and made it—in *favor* of Hitler and Nazism, no more and no less, period.

Rejoins Borgeson in *The First Century*, "Between 1930-38, just 117 of these cars were made. A few bare chassis were sold, but the great majority were finished at the company's Sindelfingen (Germany) facility. The coachwork embodied the consistent, in-house styling idiom that gave it its most prestigious expression. Wood or wire wheels were optional; pointed radiator and external exhaust flex pipe were standard.

"Early bodies had the severely vertical lines of the twenties, but body revolution was rapid in the early Thirties, and the 700 soon acquired the appearance of a decorous, king-sized 540 K."

Stated Swdish author Jan Melin in 1985 in *Mercedes-Benz Eight*, "During the 1930s, Daimler-Benz produced a number of exclusive supercharged eight-cylinder passenger cars that have gone down in automobile history as some of the world's greatest cars. They were a fantastic blend of power and elegance, and their performance soon made them legendary."

Added an advertisement line in one of the original brochures, "The 'Type Super Mercedes' is supplied with technically and artistically perfect Special Bodies to the buyer's own design and requirements."

Noted Borgeson in *Pomp and Circumstance, Darling of the Newsreels in The First Century: Portraits in Celebration of the Daimler- Benz Centennial, 1886-1986*, "When Hans Nibel took over as engineering head of Daimler-Benz in 1929, the product line held something for almost everyone, with prices ranging from a modest 6,800 Marks for the 300 Stüttgart to 35,000 for a Type S Phaeton.

"The needs of the upper middle class were served by the Nürburg range, with its six-passenger limousine priced at 15,000 Marks. Only one thing was lacking: the vehicle of ultimate luxury, of pomp, circumstance, and state...."

In 1973, a German personnel manager born in 1929 recalled when he saw Hitler once as a small boy at the House of German Art in Münich: "Then he got in his car, an open black Mercedes, the kind we had as a toy when we were children. In the catalog, it was listed as 'Führer's Mercedes.' Everyone stared. There was absolute silence, and it wasn't until he stood up that they all shouted 'Heil!'"

Continues Borgeson, "To crown the line, Nibel was assigned the task of creating the Type 770 Grosser Mercedes—Grosser meaning 'great,' but with overtones of grandeur. If price must enter the discussion, you could motor away in a 770 convertible sedan for 44,500 Marks. An additional 3,000 would provide a Roots Kompressor, and the designation K."

According to the Daimler catalog (Volume 1) 1886-1926, "The number of Daimler-Benz employees stood at its highest prewar (1939) level, with 35,123 people at work. They produced 27,793 vehicles, including the first 13 of a total of 88 cars of the 'Big Mercedes' Type 770. The chassis alone cost 30,000 RM."

Noted a German housewife born in 1911 of the Führer: "I saw him by chance on the street in Cologne. There was a long line of cars, and he was standing up in a car with those eyes that were supposed to be so sparkling. I was suspicious from the very beginning. I never could understand what all the fascination with him was about."

Asserted Borgeson, "As befitted its name, this chassis was one of the longest and imposing of its time. Except for a massive X-shaped cross member, its frame was conventional, with half-eliptic springs all around, under slung in the rear."

Noted a German teacher born in 1926, years later—in 1973—"I saw him (Hitler) in a convoy. He wasn't as well guarded as (West German Federal Chancellor Konrad) Adenauer and those people, but I'm sure his car was armor-plated. He was making an angry face...."

Stated the wife of a gas station owner in Germany born in 1916, "He drove through Friedburg in Silesia in 1942 or 1943. There were so many people he just drove through, and the people waved a little, and he waved, too, and that was all."

Attested a German writer born in 1929 of when he saw Hitler, "I was 4 ½ years old, and I wanted to be impressed. He was driving through town and was held up by a long line of children with flowers. I was pushed onto the running board of his car, and saw him just a few inches away. He was in civilian clothes. I think he was wearing a raincoat. He didn't have any charisma at all! I was really disappointed."

Wrote Borgeson, "Early bodies had the severely vertical lines of the Twenties, but body evolution was rapid in the early Thirties, and the 770 soon acquired the appearance of a decorous, king-sized 540K. A number of 770 owners were indeed royal...."

Sgt. Floyd Talbert of the U.S. 101st Airborne Division recalled to the late American author Stephen E. Ambrose that "the captors of some of the Hitler cars roared around Berchtesgaden's country roads with all the gasoline they could want—the motoring opportunity of a lifetime!"

Stated Dr. Josef Gœbbels in his diary entry of February 10, 1933, "The Leader opens the Automobile Exhibition, and for the first time publicly makes known in general outlines his ideas for the organization and promotion of German industry. They have a revolutionary effect on German employers and employed. We shall yet manage to get production going again. We only require sufficient courage to work with new methods The old ones are exhausted and effete."

In his remarks, the new Reich Chancellor referred to cars as, "Probably today's most important industry," and then proceeded to outline his ideas for promotion of it overall. His general emphasis was on new roads and a vast increase in the building of cars, both of which were accomplished within his first four years in office—just as he had promised they would be.

Although Germans had invented the car, their automobile industry really didn't grow until Hitler's commitment at the 1933 show. Another reason for the lack of rapid expansion had been the industry's over-customization of large cars, and the failure to build small ones for the average driver. This Hitler was determined to rectify. Thus, the person of the Führer was the key element for the truly phenomenal growth of the period 1933-44.

In an article published after his death entitled *The Journeys of Adolf Hitler*, Julius Schreck noted that, "Adolf Hitler's extensive knowledge of the German people is primarily the result of his travels across the nation. He desires to be among the people, and he travels by car, plane, and rail to the far sections of Germany. Traveling was much easier when Hitler was not known! Today, however, the knowledge of his motor trips spread through the villages and cities, and thousands are waiting for a glimpse of Hitler as he passes through."

Adds Jan Melin, "At the various automobile exhibitions and salons of the late 1939 season, it was noticeable that Daimler-Benz toned down the emphasis on the supercharged cars due—no doubt—to the general atmosphere of austerity brought on by wartime conditions. It concentrated instead on the smaller types, up to the 320. This was even more noticeable at the few salons held in 1940 and 1941. In Vienna in 1940, it was mentioned just in passing that the Daimler-Benz had the 540K, and in an account made available in 1940, mention was only made of the fact that cars above the four-liter class were available."

Supercharged Power

Writing in his 2005 work *Eyewitness Car*, Richard Sutton stated, "In the 1920s, many motorists owned powerful new 'sports' cars—cars made purely for the pleasure of driving fast. The sports cars of the 1920s had huge engines and devices such as superchargers to give them an extra turn of speed...

"Sports cars like these often had an impressive racing pedigree, for manufacturers were aware of the publicity to be won from success in auto racing...and technical innovations made to win races were quickly put into cars for the ordinary motorist."

In essence, the blower drove extra fuel into the engine to boost power.

General Automotives

"Creating a new car is a costly business, involving hundreds of people and years of intensive research, so a carmaker has to be confident that the car is going to sell before developing the concept far. Even before the designer draws the first rough sketch for the new car, the maker's requirements are laid down in detail in a 'design brief'—including the car's precise dimensions, how many passengers it will carry, how many doors it will have, the engine layout, the transmission, and much more.

"The route from the initial sketch to the finished car is a long one, and the design is subject to close scrutiny at all stages in the process," Sutton attests. " Several full-scale models are built—first usually from clay, then from fiber glass—and the design is constantly modified and refined. By the time the first production version rolls out of the factory, the car will work (and sell) perfectly—or so the carmaker hopes!...

"Wind tunnel testing has long been an important part of the design process. Hundreds of minor changes to the body profile may be made before the designers are finally satisfied that the car's 'drag coefficient' is as low as they can practically get it...Nearly every new car starts as a sketch on a designer's drawing board. The designer may draw dozens of these sketches before everyone is happy enough to proceed to a more detailed design drawing, or 'rendering.'

"Designs that are too unconventional or impractical tend to be abandoned at an early stage...Car designers must keep production costs in mind...The days when every car had a strong chassis and a separate coach-built body are long gone."

Coachwork Body

Continued Sutton, "As cars became cheaper and more popular, so the rich wanted more and more exclusive automobiles...Bodies were made precisely to the customer's requirements by the finest coach builders," like Erdmann & Rossi of Berlin. "The engines were large, powerful, and smooth-running, but they were not cars for the rich to drive, but to be driven in, by professional chauffeurs or drivers...Motorists were quite happy with an open tourer, providing it had a light...hood on the back to keep the dust out and set up in case of heavy rain.

"...Open tourers were often preferred to tall, closed limousines, which swayed alarmingly on corners...By 1909, most cars had a long hood running in a smooth line back from the radiator, with headlights mounted on either side...After 1909, cars usually had windshields to keep off wind and dust, but there were no wipers (until, reportedly, Prussia's Prince Heinrich—the Kaiser's younger, race car driver brother—invented them), so chauffeurs smeared the shield with raw potato or apple to help rainwater run off...Early cars carried spare tires, but no spare wheel, so, in the event of a flat tire, the driver had to jack the car up, pry the old tire off the wheel rim, put on the spare, and pump it up."

Travel Hazards

"Owning a car provided every reason for dressing up and getting equipped for touring. Indeed, protective clothing was vital in the open cars of the pioneer era. Not only was there rain and cold to contend with, but—worst of all—the dreadful dust thrown up by dry dirt roads," such as motorist Hitler still encountered in the Germany of the 1920s and '30s.

"Motorists would often come home covered from head to foot in a thick layer of muck. At first, clothes were adapted from the riding and yachting and other outdoor pursuits, but before long, a huge variety of motoring clothes was on sale," such as the leather motoring caps that Hitler and his entourage wore, and as seen in this book.

"Some were practical and sensible; others clearly for show. A motorist could easily spend as much on a motoring wardrobe as on a new car, yet the pleasures of the open road made all the little hardships and the expense worthwhile, and 'touring' became highly fashionable...Goggles and headgear [such as Hitler wore] were vital in an open car with no windshield. At first, peaked caps were popular with the fashion conscious.

"Serious drivers preferred helmet and goggles, but soon, most drivers were wearing helmets—with built-in visors, earmuffs, and even 'anti-collision protectors.'...Car advertisements made the most of the pleasures of fast motoring through lovely countryside...

"Getting lost became a regular hazard for pioneer motorists on tour. Signposts were then few and far between. One dirt road looked much like another...Sets of the new, detailed road maps [such as Hitler often consulted] that quickly appeared in stores became as vital to the motorist as a set of tools..."

Stylish Travel

"With few roadside cafes, British motorists found taking their own tea with them was a necessity—and all part of the great adventure of motoring. Since the journey could take hours—and you could be stranded anywhere—it was worth doing properly, so motorists paid for beautiful tea baskets...in leather and silver. They often came with a matching lunch basket...

"Only the rich could afford a car in the early days, so motoring picnics [such as Hitler often enjoyed] tended to be lavish." His were simpler. "The luxury shops could provide fine cutlery and glass, as well as hampers of champagne, roast chicken, and other expensive food.

"If craftsmanship was sought after in the earliest cars, and speed in the cars of the 1920s, then the 1930s was the era of styling. Beautiful body styling gave a car luxury appeal at a fraction of the cost of fine coachwork. A good design could be reproduced again and again on the production line...With huge engines and elegant bodywork, they were usually fast and always glamorous," as, indeed, was the 770K Grosser Mercedes.

"The Depression years of the 1930s may've been hard for the poor, but for the rich and famous, they were the golden days of grand touring," as, indeed, they were for Hitler and Göring, von Ribbentrop, and Speer. "The US led the way in styling, but Europe had the master coachbuilders," as Erdmann & Rossi for the Grossers purchased for Hitler and the other top Nazis.

"The best designers styled a car completely," as we shall see pictorially. "Bodies were often shaped for looks more than usefulness...Trips to the seashore were fun," and Hitler enjoyed his to the North Sea, as did Göring. "Cars of the 1930s were designed for maximum passenger space...The rear doors open backward for easy access, and the back seat extends well over the rear wheels.

"In the 1930s, carmakers began to give their cars trunks...It had up-to-date features like automatic semaphore turn signals, windshield wipers, heaters, sidelights, and headlights—all things that had been rare a few years earlier."

Trim

"While the car's mechanical and body parts make it go, it would not be a practical, usable machine without the trim: the seating, windows, tires, electrical equipment, and decoration. Most trim items are attached to the car after the rest is fully assembled...As cars traveled further, good seat design became crucial...Hubcaps are mostly for show, but also protect the wheel nuts and bearings from dirt and damp.

"Efficient generators have enabled modern cars [such as the elite 770K] to bristle with a host of electrical accessories, from essentials such as windshield wipers and heater fans, to luxuries...With tough, modern glass, cars have big, curved windows...Technology has equipped the dashboard with a growing range of instruments to measure everything from speed to brake condition."

The Engine and Other Power Sources

Continues Sutton, "Under the hood of nearly every modern car is an internal combustion engine—just as it was in the first Benz well over a century ago...The engine is a 'combustion' engine because it 'combusts' (burns) fuel, usually a mixture of gasoline and air. It is an 'internal' combustion engine because the fuel burns inside the cylinders...

"By a happy coincidence, gasoline was discovered in 1857—just two years before Etienne Lenoir built the first internal combustion engine. Most car engines have run on gasoline ever since...The spark plug may be small, but it is vital. It is the spark plug that ignites the fuel charge to send the piston shooting down the cylinder...The electric starter motor—first seen on a Cadillac in 1911—was considered a real boon for women drivers. Before the days of electric starters, motorists had to start their cars by hand...

"...The car will not run without a good electrical system. Electricity is needed to start the engine, to fire the ignition, and to power the lights, windshield wipers, and other accessories...In the very first cars, the engine was linked more or less directly to the driving wheels."

Springs and Tires

"...Cars were first given springs to cushion passengers from bumps and jolts. With the solid tires and rutted roads of the early days, springs were really needed. Pneumatic tires and tarred roads have since made life much more comfortable...Springs are far more than just cushions. A car's suspension—its springs and dampers (shocks)—is fundamental to the way it stops, starts, and goes around corners. Without it, the car would leap dangerously all over the road—which is why modern suspension is so carefully designed."

The 770K Pullman Limousine

"The Grosser Mercedes 770K Pullman Limousine was a 7.7 liter eight-cylinder giant introduced in 1938," according to George Bishop in *Classic Mercedes*.

Noted the later German author Ludwig Kosche in *The British "Göring"* in the October 1983 edition of *Wheels and Tracks* magazine, "This 770 Pullman limousine, described as 'Hitler's armor-plated Benz,' was reported to have been taken by the French 2nd Armored Division under Gen. Jacques LeClerc when it briefly occupied The Berghof...After the war, this car was shown to the public in Paris (November 1945), Brussels (1946), Geneva (May 1947), and elsewhere, including North America."

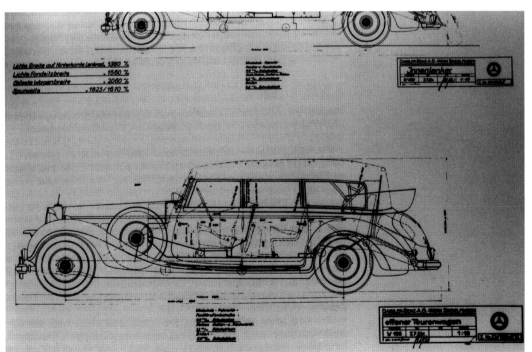

Daimler-Benz factory blueprints for the Grosser Mercedes open touring car with convertible top (hood) up. (Mercedes-Benz Albums, Library of Congress, Washington, DC.)

A left front view of the overall chassis with eight-cylinder engine without the supercharged compressor valves attached. (Roger Wychgram Collection, Aberdeen, MD.)

A Comparative G-4 chassis. (DBM.)

Above: Two good views of the rear axle suspension springs, wheels, and fuel tank of a typical Hitler Grosser. In 1973, a 51-year-old German photographer remembered that, "In 1932, the Gauleiter of East Prussia (Erich Koch) didn't even have a car yet! They were holding an election campaign, and they came to my father. He had an open 1930 Mercedes-Benz; they borrowed that, but they didn't want a driver. They'd brought their own, but the stage effects were already being used, and in this car, Hitler drove from station to station. We still have the photo: Hitler in our car." (RWC.)

The transmission and engine. (RWC.)

The Grosser Mercedes engine as seen from the front, without the honeycombed radiator grill and bodywork, showing tires and springs in this picture from an original 1930s sales brochure. (RWC.)

A good right-side view of the Type 770 Grosser/Grand Mercedes-Benz touring car model that Hitler and the other Nazi leaders made famous before and during the Second World War. (RWC.)

The *Führer* and his entourage visit an auto plant in 1933, from left to right: Schaub, three unknown men, and Hitler with unknown tour guide and Nazi aide. (Mercedes-Benz Albums, LC, Wash., DC.)

Revealing right-side views of the Grosser Mercedes' eight-cylinder engine, showing the twin compressor Supercharger pipes. Recalled a German Protestant minister at age 63 in 1973, "I stood right next to his car and looked right into the window—we weren't kept back in those days—and even then he was a loved as well as a hated man." (RWC.)

A previously-unpublished view of top Nazis at a Berlin Auto Show in the Mercedes-Benz section inspecting an engine, from left to right: a trio of Daimler-Benz officials standing at left with Dr. Wilhelm Kissel of the firm standing in the center; Gen. Karl Bodenschatz (left profile), Hitler, Field Marshal Hermann Göring (with NSKK Leader Adolf Hühnlein just visible behind him), Dr. Walther Funk, and Jakob Werlin wearing SS black overcoat. (Photo by Helmuth Kurth, Hermann Göring Albums, LC, Wash., DC.)

Hitler salutes at an annual HJ Nazi Party Congress rally before the war. In the rear seat are Hess (left) and HJ *Führer* Baldur von Schirach (right.) Note the lamp at center. Schaub stands at center in SS black.(HHA.)

At the 1935 Berlin Auto Show, Werlin (left) appears with a pensive Hitler and the NSKK's Adolf Hühnlein to inspect a new and powerful German-built engine. Just as Werlin was Hitler's insider at Daimler-Benz so, too, was he the firm's link with the highest leaders of Nazi Germany's big business, traveled widely in German-occupied Europe, and supervised the company's vast Swiss bank account cash reserves, attested author Bernard P. Bellon. There, Werlin may've been Eduard Schuelte's source for Allied Intelligence's knowledge about the growing Holocaust against the Jews, gypsies, and others. In all, Hitler as Reich Chancellor attended six annual Berlin Auto Shows during his tenure in office, each February from 1933-39. (HHA.)

An excellent aerial view of license plate IIA-19537, as the *Führer* (center bottom) strides to his waiting car, followed by Sepp Dietrich and, behind him, most likely Vice Chancellor Franz von Papen. The date is probably May 1, 1934, for the Nazis' second May Day celebration since taking office. Schreck is at the wheel. Note, too, the lined up members of the LSSAH bodyguard on either side of Hitler's path. (HHA.)

Not Grossers, but still an impressive lineup of waiting Nazi cars showing their finely upholstered seating outside the Berlin Olympic Stadium for the 1936 Summer Games. (HHA.)

A prewar scene, but previously-unpublished, from inside Hitler's car looking out. His left ear is at top upper right. (HHA.)

Propaganda Minister Dr. Josef Gœbbels (right) in an open tourer with his Fascist Italian counterpart, the *Duce's* Minister of Popular Culture Alessandro Pavolini, during Mussolini's State Visit to Nazi Germany in September 1937. (HHA.)

Another, similar—but wartime—view, taken somewhere on the German Autobahn in 1940. Kempka drives. If you look closely, you can also see the point at the rear of Hitler's cap where the gold braided strand around the top meets—but not quite! (Walter Frentz.)

The interior of a Grosser Mercedes W 150 open tourer showing a restored car's convertible top in the up position. Note the metal framework of the top, as well as the plush leather interior. (Mercedes-Benz Albums, LC.)

A good interior/exterior view of a Grosser Mercedes Cabriolet D W 07 1937 model with skirts covering the rear wheels. Visible also are the foot and armrests, leather coverings, hardwood fittings, and the convertible top's leather covering, complete with straps holding it in place. Note, also, the thickness of the door! (Mercedes-Benz Albums, LC.)

A superb interior view of one of Hitler's Grossers showing the trio of mid-car jump seats in the open position. When not used, they were folded forward against the back of the frontal seating section partition. When all seats were being used, five could be accommodated in back and two more in front, for a total of seven passengers. (M-B Albums, LC.)

Happy Ukrainian youngsters clowning around in the official car of RFSS Himmler during his tour of the conquered areas of the USSR on August 15, 1941. The SS cap/*Schirmmutze* is most likely that of Himmler's personal chauffeur, Sgt. Josef Kiermaier. (Walter Frentz.)

Hitler salutes in Silesia at the opening of an Autobahn stretch in 1936 along the Czech frontier. Note his cap on the front seat, and also the strap on the rear of the front seats' backing. (HHA.)

Through Hitler's windshield, as *he* saw the road ahead, a photo taken from behind his head and left ear. Notice, too, his frontal reflection in the windshield wiper housing at upper right, and also in the driver's rear view mirror at left, and the Mercedes' three-pointed star on the hood. Taken along the Streche Lauenburg on June 20, 1935. (HHA.)

The *Führer* didn't stand on top of the front seat when saluting, but the seat itself tilted back, as shown here. (M-B Albums, LC.)

G-4 interior update: richly upholstered, individual jump seat at mid-car. (MB Albums.)

An enduring and iconic image: Hitler giving a casual, backhanded Nazi salute from the front seat of his Grosser 770K open touring car. Sitting on the jump seat behind him is his SS bodyguard, Karl Wilhelm Krause. Note, too, the *Führerstandarte* on the right front mudguard. (HHA.)

An overall exterior view of a 1938 Grosser Mercedes parade car Cabriolet F. The superimposed numbers indicate the following: 1) 400 hp engine, 2) 20-cell tires, 3 40mm bulletproof windows, 4) Hitler's seat, raised 13 cm higher than the others; 5) his footrest, also raised 13 cm higher; 6) aluminum parts to lighten the overall vehicle; 7) spare tire and cover, used to protect the engine as well; 8) electromagnetic circuit blocking the doors, 9) manganese-treated armor plating protection from rear-fired bullets; 10) 300-liter gas tank; 11) nickel-silver radiator; 12) the *Führerstandarte/Leader Standard,* Hitler's personal flag, designed by him; and 13) overall 18 mm armor plating. (Statistics and photograph courtesy the Daimler-Benz Museum, Stüttgart, Germany.)

Mercedes production line, as seen in this previously unpublished photo. (Mercedes-Benz Albums, LC.)

List of licence plates on Hitler cars beginning with IA-148.

A) *By type and characteristic:*

148 656	Pullman limousine
148 699	Pullman limousine
148 461	Convertible limousine: crossbar between front mudguards
148 764	Convertible limousine: crossbar between front mudguards
148 768	Convertible limousine: crossbar between front mudguards
148 485	Convertible limousine: no vents under windscreen
148 655	Convertible limousine: cooling-slits in top of bonnet
148 697	Convertible limousine: cooling-slits in top of bonnet; no guards behind front bumper

3) *Registration numbers in photographic, chronological appearance:*

148 764	March 14/15, 1938	Vienna, Anschluss
148 768	September, 1938	Nuremberg, Party Rally
148 485	May 1, 1939	Berlin, May Day Parade
148 461	June 18, 1940	Munich, Mussolini visit
148 697	July 19, 1940	Berlin, Reichstag session
148 699	November 12, 1940	Berlin, Molotov visit
148 655	November 21, 1940	Vienna, Hitler's arrival at Castle Belvedere
148 656	? 1940	Sindelfingen, at time of delivery?

The "v" indicating wartime use has been found in the following registration numbers: 148 461, 148 697, 148 699 and 148 764.

List of (some) license plates on Hitler cars, beginning with II-148. (Courtesy *After the Battle.*)

A spanking new Mercedes-Benz 540 K cabriolet B underneath a portrait of Hitler in a Daimler-Benz showroom awaiting customers, an image that, today, the firm would prefer to forget. (M-B Albums, LC.)

Not a Grosser, but Dr. Gœbbels in his personal Mercedes Nürburg open touring car, license plate IA-17031, complete with SS escort guards in 1933. (Previously unpublished photo from the Heinrich Hoffmann Albums.)

An arrival by Chancellor Hitler in his Nürburg at the Neudeck home in East Prussia of the ailing Reich President Paul von Hindenburg, here greeted by the Field Marshal's son, Col. Oskar von Hindenburg, 1934. (HHA.)

Overlooking a stretch of Autobahn. (LC.)

License plate IIA-29596 on Dr. Fritz Todt's newly built Autobahn. (LC.)

Grosser Mercedes W 150 open tourer, license plate IA-148485, as seen here in a long view with all of the windows in place at the factory. Remembered one bookstore owner later, after having seen a car-borne *Führer*, "Hitler—he was this little man in a huge car, something brown in a funny pose, twisting its right arm." (M-B Albums, LC.)

In 1934, Chancellor Hitler returned to Landsberg prison after 10 years in a Mercedes-Benz open tourer for a photo taken near the city's old gateway arch, which still exists. Seen here are Hitler, Krause (seated), and two unidentified passengers. (HHA.)

A rear view of the same car, top up. Noted Jan Melin, "The hood (top) had to be high and square at the rear in order to give enough headroom in the rear seat." Recalled one German observer, a hundred people were killed in a factory explosion, and the Führer attended the funeral—"as politicians do the world over. I was 10 years old (in 1935), and it made a tremendous impression on me—Hitler with his cap, in a black Mercedes. He drove past, we stood there and cheered. No, come to think of it, we didn't cheer. A special order had been posted: No cheering—funeral—and the convoy, driving past." (M-B Albums, LC.)

A series of Mercedes "beauty shots" at the factory, tops both up and down. (M-B Albums.)

A Hitler Grosser with all bulletproof windows in place (LC.)

Hitler ascends the stone steps of a Nürnberg reviewing site for one of the annual perwarSeptember Nazi Party Congresses accompanied by (left) Interior Minister Dr. Wilhelm Frick and (right) German Labor Corps (RAD) *Führer* Konstantin Hierl. Hitler's Mercedes forms a backdrop to the scene, parked down below on the field. (Previously unpublished photo from the Heinrich Hoffmann Albums, USNA, College Park, MD.)

The *Führer* (left) shakes hands with his newly named OKW chief, Army Gen. Wilhelm Keitel. At right, wearing ceremonial sword, is Hitler's Armed Forces adjutant, Col. Rudolf Schmundt. (HHA.)

A photo skillfully air brushed by an artist to include the Mercedes-Benz hood and tri-pointed star at lower left. Here, at the 1938 Nürnberg Party Congress, are seen, from left to right: Army C-in-C Gen. Walther von Brauchitsch, Navy C-in-C Adm. Dr. Erich Raeder, Hitler, and OKW chief Army Gen. Wilhelm Keitel, with sword (M-B Albums, LC.)

Luftwaffe chief Col. Gen. Hermann Göring (center, left) shakes hands with Prince Chichibu (1902-53), the younger brother of Japanese Emperor Hirohito at the September 1937 Nürnberg Party Congress. Others from right to left are: unknown man (far left), Army C-in-C Col. Gen. Werner von Fritsch, Navy CO Adm. Dr. Erich Raeder, Göring, the Prince, an unknown SA officer, and War Minister Field Marshal Werner von Blomberg. (Previously unpublished photo from the Hermann Göring Albums, LC, Wash., DC.)

Nazi Deputy *Führer* Rudolf Hess stands between two SS officers and in front of his own open tourer. Born in Egypt, Hess was educated in Switzerland and at Hamburg, and served in the German Army in the Great War, in which he was twice wounded, and ended it as a lieutenant pilot in the Imperial German Flying Corps. (HHA.)

A previously unpublished view of Hess (center right) greeting German First World War Gen. Karl Litzmann (center left) on Adolf Hitler Plaza at the September 1934 Nazi Party Congress at Nürnberg. (HHA.)

The arrival of RFSS Himmler at Auschwitz where, on July 17, 1942, he personally witnessed the gassing of a convoy of Dutch Jews. Note his car—license plate SS-18287—at the far left, all lamps uncovered, oddly, for a wartime photo. (Polish Ministry of Justice.)

"The *Führer* often directed us to stop along the road for a picnic," adjutant Brückner would later recall. Here, the Grosser Mercedes is parked in a small wooded area while Hitler (right) and Schaub (center) and other members of the *chauffeureska* read the daily newspapers. Noted one German Labor Service youth whose unit had been marched 50 miles round-trip to salute the *Führer* at a ship launching at the port of Bremen, "We presented 'arms'—our shovels, that is—and he drove past. That was it." (HHA.)

At the gateway to The Berghof compound, Eva Braun (right) basks in the bright sunshine from the front of a Grosser Mercedes as the cars ahead of hers are admitted through to the driveway, which winds up the hill at left. The car in which she is riding, the third vehicle in this picture, generally carried the *Führer's* secretaries, and Eva rode with them on the various road outings in the surrounding countryside. (Eva Braun Hitler Albums, USNA, College Park, MD.)

Eva (right) and one of her friends clown atop their Mercedes. Note the Shell Oil sign at left rear. (EBH Albums, USNA.)

Eva (second from right in light skirt and jacket) with her friends and one of Hitler's massive Grosser Mercedes on a pleasure outing. The car is parked near a section of damaged chain link fencing. Second from left—sitting on the car's running board—is her younger sister Gretl, who in June 1944 married famous SS cavalry Gen. Hermann Fegelein. After she became Hitler's unofficial girlfriend, Eva, was at a loss as to how to tell her parents, so she planned for them to be at the Lambacher Hof on the road to Hitler's *Haus Wachenfeld* one day as one of the *Führer's* well known, shiny black Mercedes pulled up—and Eva stepped out from the rear. Incredulous, her parents asked her, "Eva, what are you doing in this car? Where have you come from? What does this mean?" She calmly answered, "I have come from *Haus Wachenfeld*," and thus the secret was out at last. Note the wooden spoked wheels. (Previously unpublished photo from the EBH Albums, USNA.)

Hitler's party about to make a wartime departure from the foot of The Berghof steps in the Grosser Mercedes. The *Führerstandarte* is clearly visible on the right front fender, with Eva seen just over the top of the hood with an RSD man at her right. Hitler's SS valet Heinz Linge holds open the door for his *Führer* at right, while Hess aide Martin Bormann prepares to enter the rear door. Standing inside in the back is the *Führer's* Naval aide, Rear Adm. Karl-Jesko von Puttkamer, while other SS officers stand outside the car. Coming up The Berghof steps in German Army uniform is Eva's father, Fritz Braun. In the car at right is Eva's older sister, Ilse. Note the panoramic view that Hitler and his guests enjoyed from the picture window and terrace of The Berghof. (HHA.)

"On the snowy steps of The Berghof, his mountain retreat, Hitler (right) descends to welcome the Polish Foreign Minister, Col. Josef Beck (fur collared coat at center), on January 5, 1939. In the meeting that followed, Hitler demanded the return of Danzig and a right of way (for cars and trains) through the Polish Corridor to East Prussia." At left is Albert Bormann, and at right center, German Foreign Office Chief of Protocol Baron Alexander von Dornberg, nicknamed "Tall Sandro." (HHA.)

As I wrote in 2007, "Chancellor Hitler (with his back to the camera) greets British Prime Minister Neville Chamberlain at 4 PM on September 15, 1938, on The Berghof's famous stone steps above the driveway, where the hood of his Mercedes Grosser can just be glimpsed at top right. The others (from left to right) are: German Foreign Office interpreter Dr. Hans Schmidt, NSKK aide Albert Bormann, and *Wehrmacht*/Armed Forces adjutant Col. Rudolf Schmundt on the way to the *Führer's* office for the second of three summit meetings during the Czech crisis that almost led to war." (HHA.)

Hitler sees off one of his prewar guests on the driveway of The Berghof, at the bottom of the stone steps. Note that the Grosser's top is up. The house seen at upper right is that of Martin Bormann. (HHA.)

As I noted in 2007, "An outstanding scenic view, looking down the steps from the top landing. Today, only the lower right portion, plus its retaining wall, is still visible. From left to right are: (center) King Carol of Rumania, von Ribbentrop, Otto Meissner, and Hitler during a prewar conference." Note the Mercedes Grosser behind them on the driveway. (HHA.)

4

Hitler's Chariots in Use

The Nürnberg Party Congress Rallies

The Nazi Party held annual, semi-annual, and even seasonal rallies of the faithful to keep their membership pumped up before and during the course of the 12-Year Reich, which was designed to last a millennium, but didn't.

The first Party Day was held in 1923, followed by German Day that same year. Another rally was held at Weimar in 1926, in which Hitler reviewed his parading marchers from a Mercedes-Benz for the first time. Afterwards, all major annual Nazi Party Congress Rallies (except for the fall Harvest Festival, which was held each year at Bückeberg) took place in and outside the gabled, medieval city of Nürnberg.

These were billed officially as follows: the Day of Awakening 1927, the Party Day of Composure 1929, the Party Day of Victory 1933, the Party Day of Unity 1934 (after the Röhm Purge), the Party Day of Freedom 1935 (celebrating Germany's new draft law and rearmament start-up), the Party Day of Honor and Freedom 1936 (commemorating the addition of the Rhineland to the Reich), the Party Day of Labor 1937, the Party Day of Greater Germany 1938 (hailing the Union with Austria and the expected acquisition of the Czech Sudetenland later that year), and the final one that was never held, the Party Day of Peace in 1939 (Germany invaded Poland, and it was simply cancelled.)

Hitler, Göring, and Speer dreamed—and even planned for—a Party Day of Victory in World War II for 1950—complete with V-1 and V-2 rocket demonstrations—but the defeat of 1945 intervened instead, alas.

These colorful, mammoth, and visually impressive rallies provided a ready made stage on which the Grosser Mercedes 770K was rolled out year after year as both Hitler's entrance vehicle and as his mobile reviewing stand, planted each September downtown on the newly named Adolf Hitler Plaza.

State Visit Venues

The shiny, black (dark blue, actually) monster cars also served to welcome and transport the Third Reich's phalanx of famous foreign visitors, both before the Second World

Standing in his Grosser Mercedes-Benz parade car, German Reich Chancellor Adolf Hitler salutes his goose-stepping, black-jacketed, white-belted *Leibstandarte/Lifeguard SS Regiment* in front of the Old Reich Chancellery in Berlin on his 50th birthday, April 20, 1939. Standing in front of the car are (left) RFSS Himmler and (right) SSLAH commanding Gen. Sepp Dietrich. (HHA.)

War and during it: Mussolini, Chamberlain, Antonescu, Daladier, Horthy, David Lloyd George, Molotov, the Duke and Duchess of Windsor, and many others as well.

The Grosser as State Gift

As I wrote a decade ago, "It is significant to note that—throughout the entire life of the Third Reich—only three Grossers were given by Hitler as presents—and that none went to his main wartime ally, Mussolini (to whom he gave an anti-aircraft railroad car instead, however)."

Marshal Karl Gustav Baron Mannerheim of Finland got one open tourer Grosser, and Generalissimo Francisco Franco of Spain received another (a Pullman limousine), as well as a G-4 cross-country touring car; Marshal Ion Antonescu of Rumania reportedly got a car as well. Hitler admired Mannerheim and Antonescu, but came to loathe Franco.

According to Swedish 770K authority and author Jan Melin, the Mannerheim car (it ended as a 75th birthday present) was ordered on June 27, 1941, by the Office of Hitler's Adjutancy in Berlin. Melin further believed that, "It was intended as an expression of Hitler's admiration for the bravery of the Finnish nation in its defense against the Russians.

"After all, Mannerheim's birthday was not until six months after the car was delivered," on June 4, 1942. On November 15, 1941, the car was driven to Berlin and delivered to the Adjutancy, then to FHQ Ft. Wolf (Wolf's Lair) at Rastenburg for Hitler's inspection, bearing SS license plate SS-02047.

Continued Melin, "Following the inspection of the car, it was driven to the German port of Stettin, and shipped from there to Vasa, a port on the west coast of Finland. This information comes from the late Erich Kempka, Hitler's chauffeur, who went with the car [ala those of Daimler-Benz during the same period] 'to deliver it and to show the Finnish chauffeur how to drive and look after it.'

"From Vasa, the car was driven to its destination, St. Michel [Mannerheim's wartime headquarters]. It was here—on Dec. 16, 1941—that the car was handed over to the Field Marshal, in the presence of several members of his General Staff. Erich Kempka and Maj. Gerhard Engel—Hitler's Army adjutant—handed over the car."

During Hitler's visit to Marshal Mannerheim to celebrate his 75th birthday on June 4, 1942, it is interesting to note that Finnish chauffeur Kauko Ranta became one of the few foreign drivers ever to be allowed to drive Adolf Hitler, either in peace or wartime. In December 1944 Ranta handed over the car keys of the Grosser Mercedes, "The finest car he ever drove."

In March 1946 Mannerheim resigned as President of Finland (having first succeeded President Rysto Ryti), and the car was shipped to Stockholm on January 28, 1947, where it was sold to Swedish buyer Gosta Sverdrup that May.

On June 18, 1948, the car was shipped by sea to New York, where it was unloaded on June 28th and later driven to Chicago and sold to buyer Christopher Janus. Since it received national coverage at its New York arrival, the car was mistakenly believed to have belonged to Hitler himself.

For a time it was displayed at the Museum of Science and Industry at Rockefeller Center, and Janus next sent it on a nationwide charity fundraising tour.

Concluded Melin, "In January 1973, newspapers all over the world reported that the Grosser Mercedes had been sold at an auction in Scottsdale, AZ. In October of the same year the car was again sold, and now the price was up to $ 176,000. At each of these sales the car was claimed to be Hitler's. Since then, prices of $500,000 have been mentioned. At the moment, the car seems to be lost to sight."

The exact same scene(from the previous page) as viewed by Hitler himself, from behind him, standing in the Grosser, and looking out. (HHA.)

Another view of the same scene, looking over from the SS band's vantage point. (HHA.)

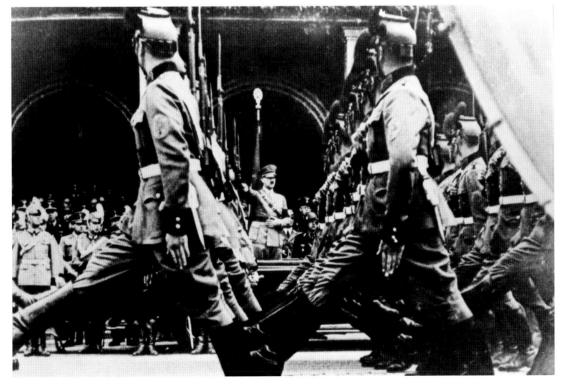

Reich Photo Reporter Prof. Heinrich Hoffmann (right) in action as he photographs Hitler reviewing an SA color guard in 1934. Saluting at left in black SS uniform is RFSS Himmler. Note the garlands atop the flagpoles, an interesting touch. (HHA.)

The German Regular Police march past their *Führer* in his Mercedes-Grosser. The view is from across the street, just behind a drum (right) of the Police band. (HHA.)

Prime Minister of Prussia Hermann Göring reviews men of the SA Regiment *Feldherrnhalle*, of which he was the honorary Colonel. SA Chief of Staff Viktor Lütze stands behind Göring in the car as the color guard goosesteps past in this previously unpublished photo. Note the snow chains on the spare tires. (HGA, LC.)

The same parade as viewed from across the street, from the crowd's viewpoint. (HGA.)

Münich Gauleiter Adolf Wagner stands in his open tourer during a review in his city. At right center are *Luftwaffe* Gen. (later Field Marshal) Hugo Sperrle and Army Gen. *Ritter*/Knight Eugen von Schobert, later killed in action in Russia. (LC.)

The same scene as viewed from a different angle, and also with the addition of a pair of Fascist Italian officials next to von Schobert, at right. (LC.)

The same review from a different angle, from behind the RAD band across the parade ground opposite Hitler's Grosser reviewing stand. Note the spades held at shoulder arms, as well as the enlarged *Führerstandarte* on the speaker's dais behind the car. (HHA.)

A trio of views of the same September 1935 event, with Hitler reviewing the RAD at Nürnberg's *Zeppelinwiese*/ Zeppelin Field. Standing in front of the Grosser are Hess, Dr. Wilhelm Frick, RAD separate unit commanders, and its overall leader, RAD *Führer* Konstantin Hierl. (HHA.)

The same event and place, but in a different year. This time, the left to right lineup is Frick, Hess, RAD unit commander and, again, Hierl, with Hitler standing in the Grosser, taking the salute, also at the Zeppelin Field. (HHA.)

A view of the *Führer* in a Mercedes tourer (not a Grosser) at the Nazi Party Day at Nürnberg in 1929. Hitler stands at rear, while SA leader Franz Pfeffer und von Salomon stands on the car's running board at center, wearing *lederhosen*/leather pants. Flowers lie on the cobblestones below and also atop the car's windshield in the down position. Outside, from left to right, at the car's rear stand Julius Streicher, Nazi publisher Max Amann (not having yet lost his left arm), an SS man, and an early SA leader. (HHA.)

The same scene from the band's viewpoint once again. This time—atop the Zeppelin stand—is the gilt gold Nazi swastika so famously blown up by the U.S. Army in 1945. Note the spaces, carried at shoulder arms. (HHA.)

Baldur von Schirach (right) salutes his passing HJ boys on Adolf Hitler Plaza in Nürnberg in September 1933 from a Mercedes-Benz parade car. The bald-headed man standing in front of the car at left is Gauleiter Julius Streicher. (HHA.)

International military attachés to German embassies salute from their vantage point in the reviewing stand on Adolf Hitler Plaza in downtown Nürnberg, accompanied by a German Army liaison officer at center. (HHA.)

As I wrote in the *Automotive News Centennial Celebration of the Car* on October 30, 1985, "During one of the annual, mammoth Nazi Party Rallies at Nürnberg, Hitler prepares to enter his limousine to take the salute of SA Stormtroopers...Hitler created a Nazi Motor Corps to transport Stormtroopers, and, later, to popularize motor travel within the Party." The man holding the door is SS Second Lt. Karl Wilhelm Krause, the *Führer's* longtime prewar personal bodyguard. At far left is Göring, wearing SA kit, while at far right Hess is seen in right profile. Note, too, Hitler's peaked cap resting on the front seat. The V on Krause's right sleeve denotes an Old Fighter of the Nazi Movement, i.e. those members who joined the Party before January 30, 1933. The date of this scene is Monday, September 5, 1938, during the last such rally before the war. (HHA.)

A superb aerial view of Adolf Hitler Plaza in downtown Nürnberg. The stands are empty, and Hitler's car hasn't arrived yet across the square in front of the buildings at left center. (Previously unpublished, HHA.)

A rare view of Julius Streicher (right) speaking from *inside* the car while Hitler rests against the car from *outside* it. Seen also from left to right are Dr. Frick, Dr. Frank, von Schirach (behind Hess), and Martin Bormann. Note, too, the rather stylistic microphones used throughout the Third Reich Period. (HHA.)

Probably one of the more famous shots ever taken of Hitler in one of his Grosser Mercedes parade cars at Nürnberg, a good detail view from the front of the hood showing the folded down windshield, pennant staff, spare tire mounted on the running board, and lamp. At left stands SA Chief of Staff Viktor Lütze and Hess. (HHA.)

Monday, September 5, 1938: from left to right, the "usual suspects" lined up for the last review, front row: Hess, Lütze, Göring, and Pfeffer und von Salomon, with Hitler in the car's mid-section, standing in front of the jump seats. In the rear are, from left to right: Krause, SA unit commander, obscured SS man, Grimminger with the Blood Flag, and Sepp Dietrich. Note the defined cobblestones. (HHA.)

Hitler salutes, framed in this scene by the 1923 Blood Flag, held behind the car by SS man Jakob Grimminger. (HHA.)

Famed German film actress and director Leni Riefenstahl (bottom) kneels down in front of IIA-19357 to direct a cameraman filming *Triumph of the Will*, her masterpiece documentary of the September 1934 Nürnberg Party Congress that still airs on television worldwide today. (HHA.)

The enduring image: Hitler, Hess, and the Grosser used as a reviewing stand. Between the two men can be seen Sauckel and Dr. Frick. According to *After the Battle,* "Years later, Hitler confided to his close retinue that 'The most difficult effort comes at the march past when one has to remain motionless for hours. On several occasions, it has happened to me to be seized by dizziness. Can anyone imagine what a torture it is to remain so long standing up, motionless, with the knees pressed together? And on top of that, to salute with outstretched arm? Last time, I was compelled to cheat a little. I also have to make an effort of looking each man in the eyes, for the men marching past me are all trying to catch my glance." (HHA)

NSKK motorcyclists with sidecars trundle past their *Führer* in license plate IIA-19357 at left, with Göring standing in front. (HHA.)

Young *Luftwaffe* officers parade past Hitler during the September 1935 event, with Hess standing in his usual spot at left. (Previously unpublished, HHA.)

Nazi Labor Corpsmen parade with shouldered spades instead of rifles; those would come later. This time, Dr. Frick has taken Hess' place at the rear of the car, again license plate IIA-19357. (HHA.)

A front view of Hitler's limousine on Adolf Hitler Plaza with the reviewing stands far behind him, in front of the church. Marching past are RAD men, with spades held at shoulder arms. Note, too, the cordon of SS security men in the middle of the square behind the car, separating it from the reviewing stands. (Previously unpublished photo, HHA.)

A trio of views of a singular occurrence: Hitler allows another Nazi official to stand in the car *with him* to review a parade, in this case SA Chief of Staff Ernst Röhm (1887-1934) at the September 1933 Nürnberg Party Rally on Adolf Hitler Plaza. Not even Göring (seen in the right photo standing outside the car at center), in front of IIA-19357, was ever accorded this privilege, and no one would ever be again, either; Hitler had learned a lesson. Röhm had been granted this rarest honor to pacify him and to keep his unruly SA in order. This was the first rally following the Nazi governmental takeover of January 30, 1933. The second and third views are close-up views of the same scene. Röhm wasn't mollified, however, so Hitler had him shot in his Münich jail cell at Stadelheim Prison by SS men Michael Lippert and Theodor Eicke on July 2, 1934. Grimminger stands at rear with the 1923 Blood Flag. (HHA.)

Waiting for the parade to begin in September 1937, Hitler chats with Göring at center. Also waiting from left to right are Hess, Hoffmann, SA unit commander, two SS men, SA unit commander, Hitler, Grimminger with Blood Flag, Göring, RFSS Himmler in steel helmet, and Pfeffer und von Salomon, the last standing just next to the *Führerstandarte* pennant. Note the reviewing stands and church at rear. (Previously unpublished photo, HGA, LC.)

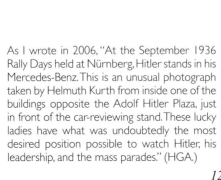

As I wrote in 2006, "At the September 1936 Rally Days held at Nürnberg, Hitler stands in his Mercedes-Benz. This is an unusual photograph taken by Helmuth Kurth from inside one of the buildings opposite the Adolf Hitler Plaza, just in front of the car-reviewing stand. These lucky ladies have what was undoubtedly the most desired position possible to watch Hitler, his leadership, and the mass parades." (HGA.)

The *Führer* salutes his passing SA flag bearers from license plate IIA-19357. In front of the car are, from left to right, Pfeffer, Göring, SA unit commander, and Lütze. (HHA.)

Tuesday, September 8, 1936: Hitler salutes SA standards being paraded past him on Adolf Hitler Plaza. Note the newsreel cameraman at right recording the scene for us—history. (Previously unpublished photograph, HGA.)

Almost the same scene, but not quite. In this view, we see Sepp Dietrich at right and, next to him, Grimminger with the 1923 Blood Flag. (HHA.)

SA reviews in Nürnberg. (HHA.)

SA standards parade past Hitler in this previously unpublished photo. (HHA.)

Below: Almost the same scene, but, again, from a different angle, showing—right to left—in front of the car, Lütze, SA unit commander, and Hess. (HHA.)

Massed SA standards (left) and flags (right) in Nürnberg. (HHA.)

A rear view of Hitler's limousine during the annual September review of Stormtroopers at the Nazi Party Nürnberg Congress. (HHA.)

A bird's eye view of tramping SA on their way to be reviewed by Hitler, whose car can be seen in the upper right of the photo at its standard spot on Adolf Hitler Plaza in downtown Nürnberg. The SA men march 12 across. Count them. (HHA.)

The same scene, but closer to the car at right. (Previously unpublished, HHA.)

Allgemeine/General SS standard bearers march past Hitler at left, with Hess and RFSS Himmler standing in front of the car. (HHA.)

One of this author's favorite 770K Grosser car shots, of license plate IIA-19357 at the September 1935 event, here published in full for the very first time anywhere. The helmeted men at left are members of Hitler's own LSSAH personal Bodyguard Regiment. Standing in front of the car are Hess at left and RFSS Himmler at right, just under Hitler's outstretched arm. (HHA.)

A good, wide-angle, panoramic view of SA flag bearers, Pfeffer, Hitler, the car (with windshield down), and Grimminger with the 1923 Blood Flag. (HHA.)

RFSS Himmler—saber in his right hand—goosesteps past Hitler's Mercedes at the head of his élite SS. Standing in front of the car are (left) Hess, (right) Göring and Pfeffer. (HGA.)

After marching past, the helmeted RFSS (right) is greeted by Hitler at the car, and then takes his place standing in front for the rest of the SS march-past. Pfeffer stands at left front. The RFSS wears the pre-1935 steel helmet. (HHA.)

As I wrote in 2007, "Hindenburg had long been enthused with cars manufactured by Daimler-Benz... It was perhaps the only thing Hitler and Hindenburg had in common. Wearing top hat and overcoat, Hindenburg sits in the back of his 1924 Mercedes Type 400 15/70/100 open tourer (not a Grosser.) The State pennant is mounted on the left front wing." He was at the time the elected Reich President. (LC.)

"Hindenburg seated next to Hitler as they arrive at the Berlin Lustgarten on May Day 1933. The Mercedes-Benz was especially ordered by Hindenburg. Based on a 400 Pullman chassis, the bodywork was completed by the Berlin firm of Josef Neuss. Hindenburg requested the roofline to be particularly high, allowing him to wear the *Pickelhaube/spiked helmet* of the Imperial German Army," as I noted in 2007. The State pennant is again in place. (HHA.)

The same car at the same event, in a different view, as the massive car turns a corner. The May Day event was the Nazis' celebration of the German labor movement. The next day Hitler struck hard, closing down all the Socialist labor union offices, seizing their membership monies, and banning them for the duration of the Third Reich. (HHA.)

On the way to church at Potsdam: in the foreground Hindenburg (with Marshal's baton), behind him Col. Oskar von Hindenburg, and Dr. Otto Meissner (Secretary of State to the President, and later, to Hitler); upper row, left to right: Dr. Dibelius (until 1961 head of the Lutheran Church in Germany), Göring (Prime Minister of Prussia), Bernhard Rust, Nazi Education Minister; and Foreign Minister Konstantin von Neurath, Hitler's first Foreign Minister. The Reich President's mammoth Grosser Mercedes waits at the bottom of the staircase, its passenger door being held open by a liveried chauffeur. (LC.)

The official State car pennant of Reich President Paul von Hindenburg on his Nürburg Type 460 Pullman limousine Grosser with his liveried chauffeur at right, a 1930-31 car. The vehicle had a coach like the Mercedes Grosser Type 770, according to *Mercedes-Benz Personal Cars, 1886-1984* by Werner Oswald, a German auto expert. (HHA.)

The Type 600K open tourer of King Abdul Aziz Sa'ud of Sa'udi Arabia, ruler of the sacred cities of Mecca and Medina, being examined in the English town of Bromley, Kent, in 1927. Note the Sa'udi crossed swords coat of arms on the plate below the honeycomb radiator grill. (USNA.)

Another superb photo that I've had in my files for 40 years that is here published for the very first time! The Nazi dictatorship under von Hindenburg's hand was sealed on June 30, 1934, when Hitler (center) purged the rebellious Nazi SA Stormtroopers in deference to the wishes of Göring, the SS, and the German Army, which threatened to overthrow the young Nazi government if something wasn't done to curb the military demands of former Army Captain and SA Chief of Staff Ernst Röhm. This photo shows, from left to right, Reich President von Hindenburg wielding in his right hand his informal Field Marshal's baton, capped by the ancient Imperial German and Royal Prussian Crown; Col. Oskar von Hindenburg behind his father, Army C-in-C Col. Gen. Werner von Fritsch; Chancellor Hitler wearing formal morning attire and carrying a top hat; Navy C-in-C Adm. Dr. Erich Raeder; and Defense (later War) Minister Army Col. Gen. Werner von Blomberg. The date is March 21, 1933, and the scene is at the Potsdam *Garnisonkirche/Garrison Church* outside Berlin, commemorating Frederick the Great, whose coffin was in the church's basement crypt, and also celebrating the opening of the new, Nazi *Reischstag*/Parliament. (HHA.)

Reich President (left) and Reich Chancellor (right) inside the former's deluxe State coach. Note the high window. May 1, 1933. (HHA.)

Spanish Generalissimo Francisco Franco's Grosser Mercedes Pullman limousine W 150, flanked by colorful Moroccan Spahi cavalrymen with lances in front of the Hotel Maria Isabel in Madrid. It was given to him in 1940 by Hitler, and is still owned by the late dictator's daughter, Carmen Franco Martinez-Bordiu. According to the American *Parade* magazine on May 20, 1990, "The automobile is in excellent condition and—according to the authorities in Madrid—rightfully belongs to the State and should be used by the incumbent King Juan Carlos in the execution of his duties. His daughter, of course, doesn't see it that way. She maintains that the Mercedes, model G-4 31 [a second car, obviously] was a personal gift to my father—not the State—and therefore belongs to our family, and we mean to retain it." (USNA.)

License plate SCV1, the official Mercedes 300 Landaulet (not a Grosser) of Pope John XXIII, here being blessed by His Holiness. Note the car's Papal pennant on the right wing. Earlier, Pope Pius XI ordered a Mercedes Nürburg—and gave it his Papal blessing upon receipt. (USNA.)

U.S. President John F. Kennedy (1917-63) stands—alá Hitler—in the rear of a Mercedes during his 1962 State Visit to Mexico City. (DBM.)

Twin views of the Mercedes Type 230G (not a Grosser) vehicle used by Pope John Paul II during his November 1980 Papal Visit to the then Federal Republic of (West) Germany, both with and without the Plexiglas enclosure, wherein the Holy Father stood during motorcades. Note the Papal pennant on the right front wing, and the license plate, BB-ST 410. Less than five months later—in 1981— the first Polish Pope of the Roman Catholic Church was shot in his Pope Mobile in Rome by a Turkish-born assassin allegedly paid by the Red Bulgarian Secret Service at the behest of the former USSR, but His Holiness survived to die a natural death instead. (USNA.)

The State Parade for Hungarian Regent Adm. Miklos Horthy (1868-1947) in Berlin on August 25, 1938, was a massive affair, as seen here. As he himself noted in his postwar memoirs, it "Was the largest that had hitherto been held. The number of armored cars—and they were not made of papier maché!—the tanks and motorized artillery taking part in that march-past, which lasted 2 ½ hours, seemed endless....'' Here, the car carrying the German and Hungarian dignitaries heads the procession at left of Mercedes open tourers as it makes its way toward the Berlin Technical High School's reviewing stand. The three lines opposite the row of cars are troops, staff cars, and trucks, and armored cars and light tanks. (HHA.)

The arrival of the Duke and Duchess of Windsor (right) at Berchtesgaden for their unofficial visit to Chancellor Hitler at The Berghof. At left is their host in a light raincoat, German Labor Front *Führer* Dr. Robert Ley. The man in the dark overcoat at center is German Foreign Office interpreter Dr. Paul Schmidt. Note the Grosser from which they have just alighted, 1936. (HHA.)

The commemoration of Adm. Horthy's State Visit to Nazi Germany of August 25, 1938. (LC.)

Adm. Miklos Horthy, Regent of Hungary since 1920 and a signatory to the Axis Pact among the nations that attacked the USSR on June 22, 1941, along with Hitler. Arrested by the Germans in 1944 for attempting to withdraw Hungary from the then losing Axis, he survived the war to become a witness before the International Military Tribunal at Nürnberg, but was not charged with any war crimes. Afterwards Horthy lived in exile, first in Switzerland and then Portugal, in which he wrote his very interesting memoirs. (LC.)

Hitler (center right) welcomes Rumania's dictator Marshal Ion Antonescu (left center) to the *Führerbau/ Leader Building* at Münich in 1940, followed by von Ribbentrop and Dr. Schmidt (left) and Field Marshal Keitel (right). Their Grosser is at the rear. (JRA.)

The massive military parade for the Hungarian Regent in front of the Berlin Technical High School at right, as Germany's newest troops—Göring's paratroopers—tramp past the reviewing stand at left. Note the pennant of the Admiral at left. Hitler's is on the other side of the elaborate canopy covering the reviewing stand. (HHA.)

The *Führer* (right rear) welcomes to Berlin Yugoslavia's Regent Prince Paul (left rear seat), and they are here seen on their way to the last and largest Nazi prewar military parade, that of June 4, 1939. Hans Linge stands on the running boards of the RSD backup car at right. Note, too, the German Navy sailors presenting arms at left. (JRA.)

A close-up of the reviewing stand, Berlin, June 4, 1939, from left to right: Göring, Prince Paul (1893-1976) executing a military salute, and Chancellor Hitler giving the Nazi Party salute as German Army troops march by. (Previously unpublished photo from the Hermann Göring Albums, LC.)

A spectacular, Hollywood-style shot of the June 4, 1939, parade reviewing stand upon which stood Prince Paul, Göring, Hitler, and others opposite the German Army band below in front of the Berlin Technical High School. Note the *Führerstandarte* at right and that of the Prince Regent at left. (HGA.)

September 29, 1937: Italian Fascist *Duce/Leader* Benito Mussolini was, without doubt, the most famous of Hitler's foreign visitors. Here, wearing the uniform of the Fascist Party Militia, the *Duce* begins his State Visit to the Third Reich of September 25, 1937, in one of Hitler's Grossers in Münich. As I wrote in 1969, "For this occasion—their first meeting since 1934—Hitler pulled out all the stops in order to impress Mussolini; he succeeded. Here, they acknowledge the cheering crowds as the official limousine moves down Münich's Ludwigstrasse/Ludwig Street. Noted author/publisher Roger Bender, 'Mussolini is visibly impressed by his welcome in Münich.'" (HHA.)

Top Photos: Note the *Duce's* Fasces car pennant in the first shot and Hitler's *Führerstandarte* in the second. Since the *Duce* was Hitler's honored guest, his pennant was flown on the right side of the car, the traditional place of honor since at least medieval times. Interestingly, neither man fell either out or over in the moving vehicle! Mussolini wears a ceremonial Fascist dagger, and sitting in the right front seat is Hitler's first NSKK adjutant, Capt. Fritz Wiedemann (later replaced by Albert Bormann), Hitler's own former First World War superior officer. (HHA.)

The Foreign Ministers of Fascist Italy and Nazi Germany ride together in the rear of this Grosser: Count Galeazzo Ciano at left and Baron Konstantin von Neurath at right. (HHA.)

The Propaganda Ministers of Fascist Italy and Nazi Germany ride together in the back of their Grosser: Dino Alfieri at left and Dr. Josef Gœbbels at right. Later, Hitler personally requested that Alfieri be named as Italy's Ambassador to Berlin, and got his wish. (HHA.)

The official motorcade on Münich's downtown Marienplatz, September 29, 1937. (HHA.)

The *Duce* and *Führer* in Grosser license plate IA-103708 after having passed under Berlin's famed *Brandenburger Tor/Brandenburg Gate* in the distance. Kempka drives. The backup car is license plate IA-16916. Note the tall pylons atop which are golden swastikas, eagles, and wreath enclosed Fasces, September 29, 1937. (HHA.)

Göring's own Mercedes Grosser Pullman limousine during the *Duce's* private visit to his country estate of *Karinhall* outside Berlin on September 27, 1937. Here, from left to right, are seen Nazi engineer Dr. Fritz Todt in left profile, Göring, the SS chauffeur, Göring aide Dr. Erich Gritzbach, the *Duce*, an unknown Fascist, Count Ciano holding his cap, and Dino Alfieri at the far right. Note the windshield wiper blades. (HGA.)

As I first wrote in 1969, "Sept. 29, 1937: The official reviewing stand on the Charlottenburger Chaussee in Berlin, for a parade of the German Army. Present are, from left to right, front row: von Blomberg [with Marshal's baton], Mussolini, Hitler, von Fritsch; back row: Göring and Raeder," the latter wearing his Naval bicorn hat in the fore and aft position. (HGA.)

The two self-proclaimed "men of destiny" meet again in München on June 18, 1940, to discuss peace terms for just defeated France. The *Duce* wears the cap and uniform of a First Marshal of Italy, of which there were but two: Mussolini himself, and His Majesty King Victor Emmanuel III of Savoyard Italy. (JRA.)

The *Duce* (left) returns to visit Hitler a year later for the München Conference on September 29, 1938. At the rear of the car is an RSD man (left) and SS bodyguard Karl Wilhelm Krause. (HHA.)

With bulletproof windows, license plate IA-148461 carries the two victors into München for a heroic welcome in 1940. Their two State pennants are affixed in their proper places on the car wings. Kempka drives, and SA adjutant Wilhelm Brückner—wearing German Army uniform—sits next to him up front. (JRA.)

The motorcade passes under Münich's famous *Karlstor/Karl's Gate*, June 18, 1940, with the lead car followed by staggered security vehicles. (JRA.)

According to Jan Melin, "Gen. Franco of Spain (left) inspecting the gift presented to him by the Germans in 1939, in the form of a G-4 *Offener Tourenwagen/Open Touring car*," his second German Mercedes. (JMA.)

The same scene today. (LC.)

El Caudillo/The Leader, Spain's Generalissimo Francisco Franco after the Second World War. (LC.)

Stated Melin in 1983, "The G-4 put to service when King Boris visited the German Führer in September 1943. The hood (top) was seldom seen on these cars." (JMA.)

His Majesty King Boris III of Bulgaria (center) leaving The Berghof after a wartime visit to Hitler (right.) At left is an unknown German Foreign Office aide. (JRA.)

Twin views of a Grosser Mercedes *offener tourenwagen/open tourer* that is here shown being inspected by Hitler and his entourage at *Wolfsschanze/Wolf's Lair*, his principal wartime military *Führer* Headquarters (FHQ) in East Prussia. This car arrived late in 1941 at Rastenburg for Hitler's inspection. In the top shot, the front of the car is well-depicted, complete with all lamp covers in place, the engine cover (hood) partially rolled down, and the convertible top (hood) in the up position. The license plate is SS-02407. In the top shot, Hitler is at the far left, but has moved closer to look under the raised hood in the bottom view. Behind him in that scene stands his Naval adjutant, Rear Adm. Karl-Jesko von Puttkamer. Note the fog lamp in bottom center. The car is a W 150 Cabriolet F. The other interesting thing about both of these shots is the above ground concrete bunker that appears at the rear. All of the *Führerbunkers*—with the sole exception of that in Berlin beneath both the Old and New Reich Chancelleries—were above and not below ground, although this always repeated myth continues to appear in otherwise informed histories and biographies of the Nazi era. (HHA.)

Mercedes passenger Marshal of Finland Karl Gustav Mannerheim (1867-1951), a formal portrait of the Marshal in full regalia, the hero of four wars: the Great War of 1914-18; the War of Liberation against the Reds, 1918-19; the Russo-Finnish War of 1939-40; and the Continuation War of 1941-44. (USNA.)

The interior of a Grosser Mercedes W 150 open tourer much like that of the Mannerheim car, showing the dashboard instruments. This photo is reproduced from a 1957 magazine article that started the current author down the long road to writing this and several other previous Mercedes books. The body number of the Mannerheim car was 200767, and its maximum weight was 4600 kg. The mudguard wings were painted black, the body a deep, dark blue. (LC.)

Another view of the same scene, but this one previously unpublished. Note the partially lowered leather radiator cover on the grill front. (HHA.)

As I wrote in 1999, "The dashboard of license plate IA-148697, as it appears today at the Canadian War Museum at Ottawa, Ontario, Canada.' (MBAlbums.) (HHA.)

On December 16, 1941, the car was handed over to the Marshal personally at St. Michel, a town that lies about 225 km northeast of Helsinki, close to Lake Saimen in Finland, where Mannerheim had established his Continuation War headquarters. Here Marshal (third from left, wearing fur cap and carrying a swagger stick) meets car (right), still bearing its SS license plate. Note, also, that the hood is partially raised over the engine. (HHA.)

A good, frontal view of the car on July 24, 1942, at the Marshal's St. Michel's field headquarters, with Finnish Army chauffeur Kauko Ranta at the wheel. Note the new license plate: SA 1. According to Jan Melin, "This stood for Suomen Armeja/Finnish Army 1, the number that Mannerheim had on all his cars." Continued Melin in his epic work *Mercedes-Benz 8*, "Daimler-Benz had sent a representative from Germany, a Herr Katzenwaddell, to be present at the ceremony, and to demonstrate the car. He was to come back to Finland three times to service the car, and to ensure that it was working satisfactorily. Also present at the ceremony was the man who was going to drive the car, the Field Marshal's chauffeur, Kauko Ranta. I first heard of Kauko Ranta in 1971, and, naturally, wanted to get in touch with him. However, it took me all of 10 years to track him down...He wrote to me in 1981." (HHA.)

The Mannerheim 770K Grosser Mercedes in the winter of 1943 with the top down and windows in place. Noted Melin, "The rear side windows (Steck Fenster in German) on an Offener Tourenwagen could not be wound down, but could be removed completely, if so wished...Field Marshal Mannerheim already had a Mercedes-Benz 320, as well as a V-12 Packard, but the Grosser Mercedes immediately became his favorite car, despite his well documented dislike of its donor. If the weather permitted it, the hood would be kept down, and Mannerheim encouraged Ranta to drive fast. [It could travel between 120-170 km/h] Kauko Ranta remembers the Grosser Mercedes as the best car he ever drove." It had no snow tires, but chains, and even a shaving razor for the chauffeur! (LC.)

"Grosser Mercedes W 150 Offener Tourenwagen, presented in late 1941 to Field Marshal Mannerheim of Finland as a gift." The license plate of this vehicle is IA-148485. (LC.)

Finnish Army chauffeur Kauko Ranta. According to Melin, "The right hand seat itself...could be tilted up to allow Mannerheim to stand up for parade inspections and suchlike. (I have never heard of Mannerheim actually doing this, as he seemed to prefer the back seat.)" (LC.)

The smiling Marshal gives a military salute from the right rear back seat of the Grosser Mercedes during the war. (LC.)

"The same Offener Tourenwagen on the same occasion," attests Melin. (Hermann Ahrens.)

States Melin, "The Finnish President (Rysto) Ryti after having picked up Hitler at the Immola Airfield on June 4, 1942 in the Grosser Mercedes W 150. They are on their way to visit Field Marshal Mannerheim." Note, too, Hitler's Focke-Wulf 200 aircraft at left on the Immola, Finland, airfield. (Mercedes-Benz Club of Finland.)

The Mannerheim Grosser license plate SS-02047 with top up and side windows in place. Note, too, that the leather radiator cover is down over the grill, just after its arrival in Finland. (Mercedes-Benz Club of Finland.)

The car arrives on the Marshal's 75th birthday on June 4, 1942, with Hitler and President Ryti of Finland to visit the Baron (who here approaches the car) on his inspection train for the occasion." The bulletproof window glass was 40 mm thick. (HHA.)

The *Führer* and German Reich Chancellor (left) and the President of Finland (right) have left the Grosser, and are seen walking the 100 yards or so to Marshal Mannerheim's train. The 770K's long hood can be seen at right. It is interesting to compare the car's height with that of the men! Hitler was about 5'9" tall. Noted the Marshal in his 1954 memoirs, "Hitler had expressed a wish that there should be no changes in the program for the day on his account, and that I was not to meet him on the airfield. This visit astounded me." (HHA.)

Wielding his new baton as Marshal of Finland (he'd been a Finnish Army Marshal since 1933), Baron Mannerheim (right) is greeted by Hitler and German Army Field Marshal Wilhelm Keitel (left) at *Führer* Headquarters on June 27, 1942. Between the two men shaking hands is Chief of the Great German General Staff Col. Gen. Franz Halder. Note the Grosser at rear, complete with wooden spoked spare tire. (Previously unpublished photo from the Heinrich Hoffmann Albums, USNA, College Park, MD.)

Following his surprise visit to Marshal Mannerheim, Hitler departs in his aircraft from Finland's Immola Airfield on June 4, 1942. From left to right are seen a Finnish Army officer, German *Alpenskorps/Alpine Corps* Gen. Eduard Dietl (the "Hero of Narvik" was killed in an air crash almost two years to the day hence in 1944), Hitler, and another Finn. SA I can be seen between Mannerheim (saluting) and Hitler. (HHA.)

The Marshal's former car license plate SA 1 being unloaded in New York on June 28, 1948, from the M/S *Stockholm*—later in a collision with the Italian pleasure cruise liner *Andrea Doria*—on which my lawyer's mother was present! The car could attain a top speed of 170 km/h. Chauffeur Kauko Ranta told Melin in 1981 that it took him four hours to wash this "Big One" properly, but that it required only three oil servings between 1941-44. (LC.)

The Mannerheim car in 1973 with Earl and Molly Clark of Lancaster, PA, sitting in it, in front of Earl's Dutch Wonderland Amusement Park on Route 30. The car appeared in the March 11, 1973, special supplement to the Baltimore *Sunday Sun* entitled *Wheels*. The article by *Sun* writer Frederic Kelly was entitled *$2.6 Million to Build Hitler's Car Brought $153,000 at Auction*, but Melin claimed this was not "Hitler's car" in the personal sense of ownership, but in reality the car was given *by* Hitler *to* Marshal Mannerheim. In October 1973, it was sold again for $176,000, and as of the writing of Melin's 1985 book its exact whereabouts were unknown. Note in this photo that the *Führerstandarte* had been affixed nonetheless! (LC.)

In America, Mannerheim's car was mistakenly billed as Hitler's, and a media firestorm ensued, as can well be imagined in the feelings of the immediate postwar era. The car toured the entire country, however, raising money for charity, as seen here, in Washington, DC in 1948. The site is just in front of the Ulysses S. Grant Monument on the West Side of the U.S. Capitol Building, from which Ronald Reagan was inaugurated President of the United States on January 20, 1981, and where the current author passed by many times during 1991-92 on my way to do photo research in the then Still Pictures Branch of the U.S. National Archives, since relocated to College Park, MD, near the University of Maryland. In 1951 Melin asserts that Hollywood's 20th Century Fox movie studio used the car in its pro-Rommel film *The Desert Fox*, starring the late, great British actor James Mason in the title role. (LC.)

5

Motorcades

According to the late German writer Ludwig Kosche in *After the Battle* in 1982, "Between 1938-43, Daimler-Benz AG of Stüttgart produced three versions of its custom built, 7.7 liter, supercharged Grosser Mercedes Type 770 W 150 convertible limousine.

"The unarmored model weighed up to 3600 kg; the armored version around 4100 kg, and both were powered by a Daimler-Benz straight eight cylinder M 150 engine rated at 145-155/230 hp. Two open exhaust pipes on the passengers' side of the bonnet showed that the vehicle was supercharged.

"The third version was the still more heavily armored 770K W 150 II, the Staatskarosse/State Coach. Why the symbol 'K' for Kompressor/Compressor indicating that the car is supercharged was not used in the designation of the first two models is not known.

"The State Coach engine—an M 150 II straight eight—was capable of developing 160/400 hp, and had a top speed of 180 kph, 10 kilometers faster than that of the first two models.

"The body incorporated aluminum mudguards, thus helping to keep the car's empty weight down to 4780 kg. This State Coach version—according to the manufacturer's data sheet— was built for Hitler, though it was by no means the only one he used. The seating capacity of these cars varied from six to eight persons, including the driver."

As I wrote on October 30, 1985, in my article *Adolf Hitler: The Dictator and His Automobiles for Automotive News' Centennial Celebration Issue*, "The gleaming black-and-chrome, armor-plated, 20-foot-long Mercedes-Benz limousines of German dictator Adolf Hitler once seemed to be the very symbol of the might of the 'Thousand-Year Reich.' His right arm outstretched in the Nazi salute, the Führer would stand in the front passenger section to review his goose-stepping minions at the giant Party Rallies of the 1930s.

"In addition, he used the cars to escort visiting fellow dictators like Italian Fascist Benito Mussolini (Il Duce/The Leader) down troop-lined boulevards. In the Mercedes he entered foreign capitals as they were occupied one after another by his invading Teutonic hordes.

"Before World War II, he motored through peaceful German villages unannounced, attracting huge crowds of people who lifted their children over their heads for him to see as he passed by.

"He is said to have logged more than 2 ½ million kilometers on the road during his career. At one time, there was an entire fleet of these expensive cars (a 1940 model is said to have cost $2.5 million to build) warehoused in the garages at the Führer's residences

A typical prewar Hitler Mercedes Grosser 770K motorcade: the *Führer's* lead car in front, followed by two staggered RSD security cars, and then those of other top Nazi dignitaries and guards. (HHA.)

in Berlin, München, and Berchtesgaden, high in the Bavarian Alps bordering Southern Germany and his native Austria.

"Ironically, after Hitler committed suicide in his underground bunker in Berlin in 1945, it was gasoline from the New Reich Chancellery garage that was used to douse and burn beyond all visual recognition the bodies of the dead Führer and his wife, Eva Braun Hitler.

"The fall of the Third Reich...saw the passing into American hands of many of those extraordinary cars. Several were brought to the US even before the war's end in the Far East. They were used as props in touring War Bond drives to raise money to fight the still-unconquered Japanese in the Pacific Theater.

"After the war, the cars and their accoutrements went on the auction block periodically as curiosity items...The prices of the cars continue to rise as the decades pass. In 1975, the brass, gold-plated license tag of one limousine was sold in New York for $4,500. The 8" by 11" plate featured the words Reichskanlzer/Reich Chancellor and Deutschland/Germany, and had a Nazi swastika on the left and a German eagle on the right." I am now—in 2009—inclined to question the authenticity of this plate.

"No doubt, as the years go by, the cars—considered mechanical marvels—will continue to make news across the country," and around the globe, too.

Noted writer Richard Grunberger in his 1971 study, *The 12-Year Reich: A Social History of Nazi Germany, 1933-45*, "The car constituted the badge of the consumer society...In 1930, when the German/American population ratio was two to one, the US had 23 million motor cars on the road, compared to Germany's half a million."

Stated the Imperial Palace Auto Collection flyer *1939 Mercedes-Benz* of its Hitler Grosser license plate IAv148451, "This 1939 Mercedes-Benz was one of several bulletproof automobiles manufactured for the use of Adolf Hitler by Mercedes-Benz.

"Although Adolf Hitler had many parade cars, this was the first bulletproof and armored car which was built for the Nazi dictator. The automobile was ordered for der Führer/The Leader and Reich Chancellor—which means Hitler—which are one and the same person.

"This automobile was ordered on Sept. 30, 1938, and delivery was made on July 27, 1939. The automobile weighs 11,960 pounds. It is 20' long, 7' wide, and comfortably carries six-nine persons. It is powered by a straight eight cylinder, 230 horsepower engine, each cylinder having two spark plugs. It will use 10 gallons of gasoline and a quart of oil for every 66 miles. Gasoline capacity is 80 gallons, and cooling system capacity is nine gallons.

"The automobile originally came with solid rubber bulletproof tires, but these have been removed, and replaced with ordinary tires with extremely low air pressure. The wheels were bulletproof."

"Hitler trusted no one. All windows are two inches thick and bulletproof as well. The floor is mine-proof. The doors—with 1 ½ " thick armor plate— weigh approximately 900 pounds each. The rear is protected by a large shield.

"Adolf Hitler was unusually cautious regarding his personal safety, and—while this car was being made—he made a trip to the factory to inspect the workmanship and personally test the armor plating with a pistol belonging to his chauffeur, Erich Kempka.. Hitler fired two bullets in the right rear quarter panel above the fender to test the armor plating." Noted Dr. Peter Hoffmann, "The plate, of course, was undamaged."

"Hitler boasted that he personally owned nothing—not a house, not a car, or even a couple of Reich Marks. This is not true, as the title to this automobile was made out

in 1939 from the Mercedes-Benz factory to der Führer and Reich Chancellor. Although Hitler used other armored cars, this is the only armored car that was made out to der Führer and Reich Chancellor."

"This is the very automobile that—on June 18, 1940—depicted Hitler and Mussolini both standing up and riding in this automobile in München, Germany. This is also the same automobile that Hitler rode in the Berlin victory parade on July 6, 1940. The pictures of the parade will attest to the fact that this is that same automobile [see color section]."

"The right front seat where Hitler either sat or stood, you will see that the seat folds back, allowing standing room at a higher elevation, giving Hitler a taller appearance, as he was a rather short man. There is a compartment in front of Hitler's seat where a pistol was concealed." Noted Dr. Hoffmann, "The Grossers could go up to 75mph top speed."

"The Great Mercedes designed for State affairs is also designed for getaways. Six gears forward; six tons in motion. This mechanical beauty is not a display to glorify Adolf Hitler, an egotist who demanded the best. This Great Mercedes represents the genius and craftsmanship of a clever people, many of whom were slaves at the time that it was built.

"Beneath and on the underside of the dashboard are the signatures of 56 people from the Mercedes-Benz factory who personally signed their names as having worked on this automobile.

"This Great Mercedes is a motor car which made mechanical history, but now remains a symbol of tyranny that few will ever forget. Adolf Hitler's personal touring car—which now stands gleaming before you—is a part of history.

"Some say because of its history, it should never be shown. Others say it is for this very reason it should never be forgotten. This Mercedes-Benz—a thing of beauty for its mechanical perfection—remains a symbol of tyranny mankind must never be allowed to forget."

Did you ever see Hitler?

In 1973, German author/editor Werner Kempowski asked Germans of the World War II era generation a single question—"Did you ever see Hitler?"—and recorded their answers. Many of them centered on or mentioned the cars, and a selected sampling follows.

"He stood in his car in his famous pose, held onto the railing (?) that was attached there. There were flags everywhere, flower garlands, and so on. Officially, everything had been set up."

"Once, before 1933, only very briefly, in Magdeburg, in the car. They were stoning him—Reichsbanner; Magdeburg was Red. He never came back to Magdeburg."

"We were prepared for his visit, so we were ready to be impressed...He put on a real show, as we understand the word today. You can show off a person so that he seems just the way you want him to. Now that I have some distance from the event, I'd say it was all a show. We'd been prepared for it in the Hitler Youth. He drove past, and we were allowed to shake his hand. At the time, we were thrilled." The witness was 14 in 1935.

"He drove through during an election campaign. There was a large crowd...First came the Escort—up front as usual. Then he arrived in his Mercedes, stood in front, over to the right. He was wearing an overcoat and a belt. He stopped, hailed the crowd a few times, and drove on...I still remember how he said, 'This is a picture I see everywhere I go,' or something like that. He meant all those people who were cheering him: blah, blah, blah."

A German architect born in 1919 said: "I saw him in Magdeburg. I was 13 and marched with my mother and brother to City Hall where the great Führer was supposed to speak. That was in 1932, and then the car was stopped on the way there, and they tried to beat him up. They transmitted the speech from City Hall, and my mother said during the broadcast, 'I don't like this at all! There's going to be war if that fellow gets into power.'"

"Once—standing in a car—but he looked repulsive, not attractive, not what you'd think of as the father of the country—God, no!'"

"He stood up in his car—that was impressive. The whole getup was impressive. He was already a symbol—even then.'"

"Just then, a convoy of cars drove through the street, and my father said, 'See, they're coming.'...He was here during an election campaign. 'He's just another camp robber,' my father would say, or 'Here he comes again in his shit-brown uniform!'"

"The older women were moaning as if the Savior were coming; to my shame, I have to admit that I cheered along with the rest."

"Hitler? In person? All right. Yes, once in Hamburg, and with a lot of pomp, while he was driving through, waving of hands. The screaming was incredible. 1936...I stood in back thinking, 'Why are they screaming like that?' because at home I'd met a man—a blacksmith—and he said, 'These people with the brown boots, they're wading in blood. The world is going to choke on it for a long time to come.'"

"I happened to be standing there in Kempten next to a glazier. Hitler was going to speak in the animal breeding hall. He drove past us in a car. You can't see too much in that kind of a situation. In any event, my neighbor made some negative remarks, and there were a couple of small fights. I don't know who they were: Party members or friends, but it ended up peacefully. I just saw him drive past...."

Stahlberg's View
Jewish-German Alexander Stahlberg recalled in his superb postwar book *Bounden Duty: The Memoirs of a German Officer, 1932-45*, of Hitler's 50th birthday on April 20, 1939: "Then came the great moment when the birthday boy drove by, standing in his big, black 7-liter Mercedes. The good company into which I had so successfully insinuated myself rose—as is proper on the arrival of a Head of State—and saluted in silence (so did I). I did, indeed, have a wonderful seat, only a few meters away from the great man in the brown uniform with the red swastika armband and the ill fitting boots.

"The weather was wonderful, real 'Führer's weather.' After that, what marched or rolled past us—hour after hour—or roared overhead from the direction of the triumphal column (industrially photographed from our stand) could have had quite an overwhelming effect. The military attachés around me were impressed.

"What was typical of Germany's policy was, of course, the immoderate character of this display. It was quantity that was intended to impress, and it became not only wearisome, but totally 'un-Prussian,' since less would have meant more."

An Olympic Moment
"They were assigned standing room in the middle and upper galleries of the stadium.

"At 3 PM, a cavalcade of heavy, black Mercedes-Benzes swept out of the Reich Chancellery: first government ministers, then International Olympic Committee members [this was on August 1, 1936] and, finally, the Führer himself, dressed in brown military uniform, wearing the Iron Cross, and standing upright in the open top car next to his driver.

"Hitler's left hand, encased in a kid glove, rested upon the top of the windscreen, his right arm returning—in a peculiar, limp manner—the Nazi salutes from the crowd as the procession made its way from Wilhelmstrasse/ William's Street along the Via Triumphalis.

"To cries of 'Heil!' it swept through the Brandenburg Gate—from which hung yet more huge swastika and Olympic banners—and into Unter den Linden. The streets were lined with the military—including members of the National Socialist Motor Corps—Storm Troopers, and special National Socialist (Nazi) guards who kept back the thousands packing the pavements.

"More fortunate onlookers had gained vantage points from windows along the route, and waved flags and handkerchiefs. As the procession passed by, a wave of applause swelled from each section of the crowd—and always there were the Nazi salutes flung skywards."

The Führer on Driver Heinrich Hoffmann
Hitler once amused his table company by describing a drive with Hoffmann in the 1920s: "Hoffmann had bought a new car—a Ford—and he insisted that I must try the car out with him. I said, 'No, Hoffmann, I'm not going for any drive with you.' But he kept pestering me, so finally I gave in, and we set out from Schellingstrasse.

"It was already evening, it had been raining, too, and Hoffman went tearing round the corners like an idiot, almost ran into the corner of a building, ignored street junctions.

"'Hoffmann,' I said, 'watch out, you're driving like a madman! This is terribly dangerous.'

'No, no, my Führer, it just seems that way to you because you haven't had a drink. If you'd put back a good glass or so of red wine like me, you wouldn't notice a thing!'

"At that, I got out, and I never went for a drive with him again."

Press Secretary Dr. Otto Dietrich's Travelogue
"Along the road between Stettin and Pasewalk 10,000 youths had been gathered in the 10 kilometer distance between these cities, to wave at the Leader as he passed through. Storm clouds and rain made the waiting unpleasant, but no one left," as he recalled in his excellent 1955 memoir *Hitler*.

"As the cars of his escort appeared, small children from the group ran forward to greet Hitler with waving flags. The Hitler Youth itself lighted flares of red, blue and green, and over 100 children encircled the Führer's car. They jumped on the running boards, crawled over the radiator, and peered into the windshield to catch a glimpse of the man. After spotting his car, the children joined hands and danced in the streets.

"'This is a holiday,' a woman was heard to say in a crowd," Dietrich recalled in 1936, "and certainly she was correct...A crowd assembled to see the Führer filled with hope, trust, and faith. The women—especially—honor Hitler, for they know that, because of him, their unemployed men have been given jobs...

"When the Führer visits a city" he recalled of 1936, "the city takes on a festive appearance and flags fly from the windows and awnings. When the Leader appears, arms rise, there is laughter and crying, and outbursts of joy and anticipation are heard...When Hitler is touring through a city, the street is filled with people waiting. Many are students who desire to see his face; everyone wants to greet him—whether man, woman, or child...."

"On a highway, two farm workers were walking in good spirits to a nearby farm center. They were singing folk songs as they walked, and they paid little attention to a group of automobiles which passed by them.

"'They have it made,' said one worker to the other. 'They will be there much quicker than we!' No sooner had the words left his mouth, when a car in the entourage stopped and gave the two a ride. When they learned they were riding in Hitler's motorcade, they were marble-eyed, yet nothing about the scene was unusual.

"It was common for the Führer to tour farm centers and find out first hand how his programs were being administered, and it was common for his escorts to offer rides to people walking along a road. When they reached the farm center, the cars stopped and the Führer talked with many workers about the efficiency of the organization.

"As he was leaving, he asked one of the two men who had been given a ride if he had a coat. 'I have no civilian coat, Mein Führer/My Leader,' the farm worker said, noticing the rain clouds that the Führer had seen. 'I have been unemployed for a long time.' The Leader immediately grabbed a green jacket from the car, handed it to the worker, and left before the startled worker could offer a 'thank you!'"

One must grant Hitler that he had a winning politician's magic touch.

Albert Speer Remembers...

On October 11, 1946, prisoner Albert Speer noted in his secret jail cell diary "The automobile rides together" that he took with Hitler both before and during the Second World War. In his entry for September 13, 1962, he recalled in his Spandau Prison diary that he'd had a dream involving an automobile as well.

On February 15, 1948, he recollected that in the summer of 1936, Hitler "Greeted me with the news that we were going to drive to Augsburg." After touring the town opera, "Outside, meanwhile, thousands of persons had gathered, a seething mob that hailed Hitler enthusiastically. The SA—which had been called in—had difficulty opening a lane so that we could drive at a snail's pace to the hotel," Speer wrote, wistfully.

On November 24, 1949, Prisoner #5 (convict Speer's prison name until his release in the fall of 1966) remembered that, "Bormann was ordered to send a chauffeur to Münich to buy a copy of the book for each one of us." In the very next day's entry, the diarist recalled, "Without Hitler, I drove to Obersalzberg with the family in my BMW, painted wartime gray."

On February 20, 1950, he stated, "My wife brought with her two handsome flannel shirts [during a prison visit]. How a fine article of clothing intensifies one's sense of self. Formerly, I used to take the wheel of my 5-liter sports car with the same feeling. Now a shirt does it."

On May 1, 1952, #5 reminisced about a wartime walk alone with his sometime rival Hermann Göring: "His many economic ties with...such firms as General Motors would undoubtedly help him after the war"; they didn't, however, and he committed suicide to avoid being hanged as a convicted war criminal by the Americans.

Writing on April 16, 1955, Speer asserted, "Ten years ago today—four days before Hitler's last birthday—Lt. Col. (Manfred) von Poser, my liaison officer to the General Staff, awakened me soon after midnight. We had arranged to drive to the Oder (River) breach in order to watch the last decisive offensive against Berlin" by the steamrolling Red Army.

On December 30, 1957, he wrote of the approaching defeat of Germany toward the end of the war, "Automobiles, planes, technological comfort would cease to exist for

Germany after this breakdown." On March 19, 1963, he wistfully noted of his childhood, "The family's new Benz touring car," even adding, "(16/40 hp)."

On October 20, 1947, Speer penned this interesting entry on Nazi intrusion into the internal corporate machinations of Daimler-Benz: "There was the question of a replacement for Dr. (Wilhelm) Kissel, the deceased General Manager of Daimler-Benz. The Board of Directors chose Dr. (Wilhelm) Haspel, although Himmler and Franz Xaver Schwartz [the NS Party Treasurer] were trying to get rid of Haspel and two other directors of Daimler-Benz, all of whom had Jewish wives. After ascertaining that Dr. Haspel and his associates were doing a fine job of running the company, Hitler refused to do anything against them; and so it remained until the end of the war.

"On the other hand, I remember that even in peacetime Hitler would occasionally declaim against the ownership of securities... 'One of these days, I'll sweep away this outrage and nationalize all corporations,'" good testimony that most likely—had the Third Reich won World War II—the victorious Führer would've hearkened back to the Socialist roots of his Party program, just as Martin Bormann and the Drs. Ley and Gœbbels always urged him to do.

In his final postwar book of three, Speer noted of an October 1952 entry: "Kammler and Saur reported to me in strong tones about the delay in transferring the Bavarian Motor Works [today's BMW car combine] to underground workshops in Alsace," toward the end of the war.

Did Hitler Ever Learn to Drive?

As I told *The History Channel's* series *Automaniac: The Cars of World War II* in its segments on the Führer's cars, "The answer is, yes, he did, but he never drove."

This is what he, himself, said on two different occasions to his intimates at Führer Headquarters. The first instance is on the night of February 3-4, 1942: "The first thing I did on leaving the prison at Landsberg on December 20, 1924, was to buy my supercharged Mercedes. Although I've never driven myself, I've always been passionately keen on cars.

"Adolf Müller had taught me to drive all right, but I knew that at the slightest accident, my conditional liberty would be withdrawn, and I also knew that nothing would have been more agreeable to the government."

On the 10th he added, "Adolf Müller's the man to whom I owe the fact that I understand the art of driving a car...Since he was going to Wurzburg to buy a rotary press, Müller suggested that I should come with him...When he told me he would himself drive his car, my first reaction was to inform him that I wouldn't come with him.

"'Get in,' he told me, 'and you'll learn what it is to drive a car.' I honestly confess that the journey was a revelation to me. Unlike most people, I'm always ready to learn... Müller opened my eyes to an infinite number of small details that escape most drivers. Every pedestrian who is installed behind a wheel at once loses his sense of consideration to which he is convinced he is entitled whilst he is a pedestrian!

"Now Müller never stopped thinking of the people on the road. He drove very carefully through built up areas. He believes that anyone who runs over a child should be put in prison at once. He didn't skirt the edge of the road—as many people do—but instead he stuck rather to the top of the camber, always mindful of the child who might unexpectedly emerge.

"When he wanted to pass a car, he first of all made sure that the driver of the car in front of him had taken cognizance of his intention. He took his curves cleverly, without making his rear wheels skid, and without sudden spurts of acceleration—all gently and flexibly.

"I realized that driving was something quite different from what I'd hitherto supposed, and I was a little ashamed at the comparisons that forced themselves into my mind. During that journey, I made two decisions: I'd buy a Benz, and I'd teach my drivers to drive."

There you have it, "straight from the horse's mouth," so to speak. In *Mein Kampf/My Battle*, published in 1925 (and still in print today, remarkably), Hitler called American automaker Henry Ford, "A single great man," and in 1938—for Ford's 75th birthday—awarded him the Grand Cross of the German Eagle, "the highest honor the German government could bestow upon a foreigner," according to Gerald Leinwand in *1927: The High Tide of the 1920s*.

Adolf Müller (1890-1944): The Führer's Driving Instructor
Müller was, like Hitler, a wounded veteran of the Great War of 1914-18, in which he'd lost most of his right leg in combat. A lieutenant general in the Nazi Storm Troopers, Müller was also one of the few ranking Nazis who called Hitler by his first name, and held several top posts in Bavaria until his death.

Miscellaneous 770K Aspects
Politicians—especially top Nazis—rode in 770Ks, as well as movie stars, bankers, sports champions, businessmen, doctors, lawyers, industrial tycoons, and basically anyone else who could afford one.

The 770K is the car most identified in the public mind even today with Hitler and his Nazis during the 12 years of the Third Reich. It was used for parades, military and Party reviews, official receptions for foreign statesmen like Mussolini, diplomats, and entries into German cities, towns, and villages. Its successor was the G-4 cross-country touring car used by the Führer to enter the occupied cities of Vienna, Prague, Warsaw, and Paris during the years 1938-40, and as shown in *Volume 1* of *Hitler's Chariots*.

How the Famous Mercedes Logo Evolved
The famed Mercedes-Benz logo—the renowned three-pointed star encased in a circle—is the world's longest-lived automotive symbol, registered in 1909. The Rolls-Royce Flying Lady came next, in 1911, and was registered in 1921.

The original star was on the Daimler family home. One day father Gottleib Daimler told his sons Paul and Adolf that "A star shall rise from here, and it will bring blessings to us and to our children." It was that star that was registered in 1909 as the company trademark, along with the name of Mercedes.

Meanwhile, the Benz Company trademark was a laurel wreath. After the 1926 merger of the two firms, the wreath was placed around the three-pointed star until 1937, when it was replaced by the plain star and ring around it that remains to this day.

Finally, the late mechanic Charlie Stitch of Grand Gorge, NY, in the Catskill Mountains, claimed to have devised the idea of placing the ring around the star and a stand to carry it on the radiator cap above the honeycombed grill. The Mercedes factory in Germany, he asserted, formally adopted his idea in 1927.

Hitler Crossing Germany
Germany is a country about the size of the American state of Wisconsin. Hitler drove across virtually every part of it.

"On Oct.ober 25, 1934, *Luftwaffe* Gen. Hermann Göring waves from the rear of a Grand Mercedes 770K at Wesermünde, on his way to memorial services for dead German fishermen. The car is license plate IIIA-33912, registered in Stüttgart," as I wrote in 1999. (HGA)

SS bodyguard 2nd Lt. Karl Wilhelm Krause, nicknamed Hitler's *Schatten*/Shadow, 1911- . (CER.)

As I wrote in 1999, "Just as his later boss, Hess, served part of his early Nazi career as a sometime bodyguard/chauffeur for Hitler, so, too, did Martin Bormann drive Rudolf Hess, as he is seen here in a motoring cap and goggles at the wheel of a Mercedes open tourer, its windshield down. Next to driver Bormann (looking unhappy in this role), is Frau/Mrs. Hess, the former Ilse Pröhl. Behind Frau Hess is her husband Rudolf, also wearing a motoring cap, as is his secretary in the back seat, Hildegard Fath. She sits next to Hess' early mentor, Prof. Karl Haushofer, the famous geo-politician. Rudolf Hess sits on the car's jump seat." (Hildegard Fath.)

Twin views of Göring's arrival and departure from the Berlin reviewing stand at the annual Heroes Memorial Day commemoration on March 13, 1938, just after he was named the sole active duty German Field Marshal. In the top photo, Göring wears *Luftwaffe* uniform and steel helmet. His Grosser is parked to the left of the reviewing stand. Göring raises his new baton [today at the U.S. Army's Ft. Benning, GA, Infantry School Museum] in salute. Mercedes open tourers are parked across the street. In the bottom photo, the Marshal departs in the same vehicle, but with a change of lighter headgear: a cap for the helmet," as I noted in 1999. (HGA.)

Wearing Republican top hat and tails, Dr. Josef Gœbbels shakes hands from his Grosser, 1933. (HHA.)

Far Left: From a seated position, Dr. Josef Gœbbels renders a casual, backhand Nazi salute from his W 150 Mercedes (not a Grosser) license plate IA111, of Berlin registry, in 1939. (HHA.)

Near Left: Now standing, Dr. Gœbbels gives the same style salute from the same car, flanked by a pair of German Regular Police on foot. (HHA.)

Below: "Security for the Führer when traveling by car, showing Arrival, Stop, and Departure." (Dr. Peter Hoffmann, *Hitler's Personal Security.*)

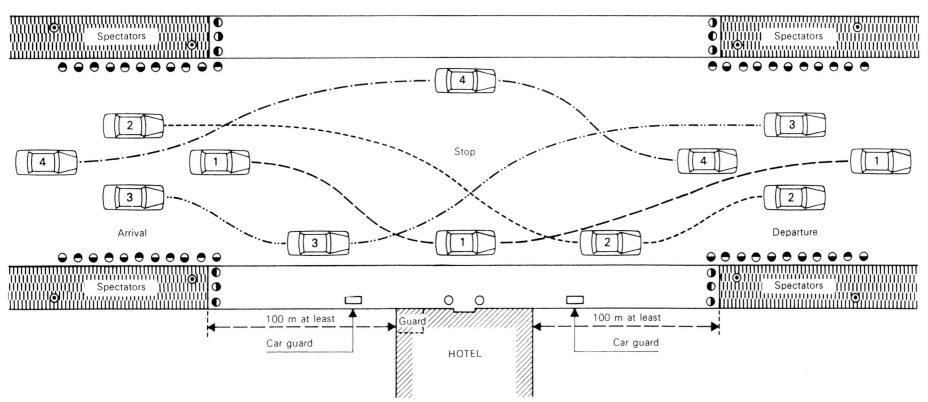

Security for the *Führer* when travelling by car, showing Arrival, Stop, and Departure

1 *Führer's* car
2 and 3 *Führer-Begleit-Kommando*
4 SS leaders

◯ ◯ Double sentry
◉ Plain-clothes guard (criminal-police or SS)
◐ SS men facing this way

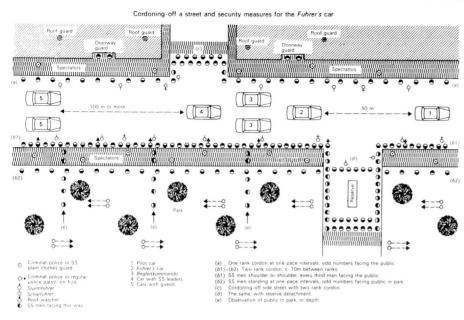

Cordoning-off a street and security measures for the *Fuhrer's* car

◎	Criminal-police or SS plain-clothes guard	1	Pilot car	(a)	One-rank cordon at one-pace intervals, odd numbers facing the public
◐	Criminal-police or regular police patrol, on foot	2	*Fuhrer's* car	(b1)–(b2)	Two-rank cordon, c. 10m between ranks
◑	*Sturmfuhrer*	3	*Begleitkommando*	(b1)	SS men shoulder-to-shoulder, every third man facing the public
◒	*Scharfuhrer*	4	Car with SS leaders	(b2)	SS men standing at one-pace intervals, odd numbers facing public in park
◓	Roof-watcher	5	Cars with guests	(c)	Cordoning-off side street with two-rank cordon
◔	SS men facing this way			(d)	The same, with reserve detachment
				(e)	Observation of public in park, in depth

"Cordoning off patterns for SS cordons, 1937" for Hitler's prewar Grosser parade routes. (Dr. Peter Hoffmann, *Hitler's Personal Security*.)

"Hitler's convoy leaving Bad Wiessee after the arrest of the SA leaders on June 30, 1934. Hitler is riding in the passenger seat of the first car; seated behind him is Gœbbels (in the light colored coat)." (Domarus Archives.)

An excellent aerial photo of Hitler's motorcade, open tourers all, seen in a typical *Führer* arrival. The *Führer's* car—and that behind his to the right—are both Grossers, and behind all three vehicles at the lower left, with a movie camera atop, is a Pullman saloon car. The way Hitler's immediate protection in a motorcade was organized, a security car was supposed to be 50 yards up front, ahead of his (and thus not seen in this photo). Two security cars would be immediately behind the Leader's car, as here; and behind them, 100 yards back, would be two more security cars. The security cars would weave in and out of each other's paths to confuse would-be assassins," as I wrote in 1999. (HHA.)

A spectacular aerial view of the *Führer* sitting opposite chauffeur Schreck passing an SS honor guard above and SS policemen below holding back the crowd (1934) with the car windshield in the down position. Riding in back are Brückner (left) and a *Luftwaffe* officer at right. (HHA.)

Hitler receives a floral bouquet from a woman (left) during a typical 1938 *Führer* motorcade, followed by a trio of cars packed with RSD bodyguards. (HGA.)

A good side view of a 770K Grosser in transit. Hitler salutes in front, Kempka drives, and SS Krause turns away from the lens in the mid car jump seat, as does Brückner in the rear seat, looking at an unidentified Army officer. Note, too, the wooden spoked wheels. This shot shows Hitler inspecting the newly completed Olympic Village in June 1936 in a W 07. The village was where the global athletes lived while at Berlin for the Summer Games. (HHA.)

Hitler opens a 1936 section of engineer Dr. Fritz Todt's *Autobahn* superhighway. (HHA.)

The April 16, 1943, arrival of Hungarian Regent Adm. Miklos Horthy on Hitler's right in the rear of a Grosser with an RSD man running behind on the driveway (right) of Klessheim Castle in Austria. At left, Hitler SS valet Heinz Linge runs to open the car door for the two leaders. The nighttime wartime lamp covers are affixed, the bulletproof windows are in place, and an unknown man sits next to driver Kempka. (HHA.)

License plate IIA-19357 about to break the ribbon for a 1936 *Autobahn* opening. (HHA.)

The Grosser Mercedes in a stretch of the newly opened *Autobahn*, with chauffeur Schreck driving. In the rear seat is engineer Dr. Fritz Todt, and Wilhelm Brückner (turning away) is in the right mid-car jump seat, with an unknown man across from him. Note the wooden spoked wheels. (HHA.)

The same car, occasion, and passengers (1935), as the *Führer* salutes. (HHA.)

License plate II-A22061 heading an *Autobahn* opening motorcade. (HHA.)

Part of the motorcade: license plate IIB-120124 (at left) and IIA-19357 at right. (HHA.)

License plate IIA-19357 leads the way again in another opening. (HHA.)

Chancellor Hitler and two RSD men, standing, with an unknown SS driver at the wheel. (HHA.)

"Hitler standing in his limousine outside the Rhine Hotel Dreesen," 1938. Kempka drives. Seated in the mid-car jump seats are Martin Bormann (left) and Julius Schaub (right); in the rear are Wilhelm Brückner (left) and Rudolf Schmundt (right.) Note, too, the LSSAH sentry presenting arms at center. Hoffmann stands outside the car at right, wearing brown peaked cap next to the helmeted SS man. (HHA/John Toland.)

"Hitler—en route from the airport through downtown Nürnberg—rides past admiring Party members and supporters in a black (sic) Mercedes touring car. This snapshot was taken on September 4, 1934, the opening day of the Reich Party Day celebration." (Courtesy C.G. Sweeting.)

Grosser license plate IA-148768 with Hitler standing and Kempka driving, Schaub at right rear, as General SS men hold back the crowd: one man facing inward, the next out—standard Nazi *Führer* security format. "I am in the midst of my people," asserted Hitler in his March 26, 1938, speech at Königsberg. (HHA.)

Hitler's Chariots Vol. 2: Mercedes-Benz 770K Grosser Parade Car

A crucial moment for the *Führer's* personal security as his Mercedes-Benz 770K Grosser slows down for a turn. Hitler and his guest Mussolini (standing) brace for the turn, while the security men both surround his car and are in the follow-up vehicle as well—as with JFK at Dallas on November 22, 1963. (HHA.)

Hitler Youth boys salute their *Führer* at the Nürnberg Stadium, September 1936. Hitler turns to acknowledge their lusty *"Sieg Heils!/Hail Victory!"* as Kempka drives. In the rear compartment are HJ *Führer* Baldur von Schirach (left) and a balding NS Deputy *Führer* Rudolf Hess. The latter two men spent 20 years in prison together after the war, both at Nürnberg and at Spandau, outside Berlin. Note the shiny black leather convertible top cover at the rear of the 770K. (HHA.)

The enduring, iconic image: Adolf Hitler—*Führer* and Reich Chancellor—standing in the front of his 770K Grosser Mercedes. In the second shot Schaub sits in the rear. (HHA.)

The enduring, iconic image: Hitler gives a formal Nazi salute from his Grosser, cap in hand, before the HJ in a stadium at Nürnberg. (HHA.)

"Hitler inspects the General Göring (Police) Regiment," the genesis of the later Hermann Göring *Luftwaffe* Airborne Division, in license plate IIA-19357, of München registry. Note the truck-mounted machine gun at left. (HHA.)

"This is not a Volkswagen kit car. It is Hitler in his Mercedes limousine as he tours the nearly completed Volkswagen factory" at Wolfsburg, Germany, 1939. Kempka is at the steering wheel, while at left— outside the car—stands Dr. Ferdinand Porsche (left) and Heinz Linge (right, in SS black.) (HHA.)

"Hitler arrives in Salzburg, Austria, in the first week of April 1938," campaigning for Austrian popular voting support of his earlier annexation of the country to Nazi Germany the previous month. He got it. (HHA.)

BDM (League of German Maidens) girls clap at Hitler's arrival in a stadium. (HHA.)

Hitler, the tribune of a nation (1939), on the eve of history's greatest war—to date—giving his secondary, casual, backhanded salute. (HHA.)

Hitler returns the salute of Nazi Party members at the HJ stadium rally at Nürnberg with Hess (left) and von Schirach (right) riding in the back of his Grosser. (HHA.)

The slogan on the ceremonial archway reads, "Victory to the Leader," as Hitler's Grosser open tourer enters Augsburg on November 24, 1937, for the celebration of the Nazi Party's founding. The car is Münich registered license plate IIA-37305. Note, too, the second Grosser at right. (HHA.)

The *Führer's* motorcade wends its way through a crowd in 1934 as SA Stormtroopers hold the people back. Black uniformed SS security men occupy the car behind his, and standing is Reich Photo Reporter Heinrich Hoffmann. Note the Mercedes three-pointed star emblem on the rear of this car, and the hood of the third car at the bottom of the picture. (HHA.)

A good rear view of one of Hitler's 770K Grossers in which the *Führer* stands and salutes from the right front passenger seat, his customary post. German Army regular soldiers hold back the Münich crowds, 1940. The license plate—IIB-170135—is Münich registered. Note also the three-pointed star of the follow up car (lower right.) (HHA.)

A Nürnberg arrival, with Schreck at the wheel and Schaub at right rear. (HHA.)

As I wrote in 1999, "Hitler stands and" gives his trademark casual Nazi backhanded salute "to the crowd in Münich, March 16, 1938." As ever, the watchful Krause sits in the mid car jump seat behind his charge as Kempka drives, and an unknown helmeted officer sits at right rear. The car is license plate IA-103708. (HHA.)

As I wrote in 1999, "Hitler's arrival at the Berlin Lustgarten in Grosser Mercedes W 07 open tourer license plate IIA-19356 in 1936. Note the Zeiss headlamps and the red searchlight on the left hand side of the car, which were on Reich service vehicles. The armored 770K weighed five tons and had hidden small arms and ammunition stored aboard to thwart attempts at a possible roadside ambush or assassination attempt. The occupants are, left to right, in the front Hitler standing and Schreck driving; in the middle Dr. Gœbbels and adjutant Julius Schaub; in the back Dr. Robert Ley and adjutant Wilhelm Brückner." According to *Eyewitness Car,* "Night driving today is relatively safe and easy, thanks to the power and efficiency of modern car lighting, but in the early days, lighting was so poor that few motorists ventured out on the road after dark....Special lights were soon developed, running first on oil or acetylene gas, then electricity. Yet for many years lights were considered to be luxury accessories. It was not until the 1930s that bright electric lights were fitted as standard on most cars." (HHA.)

An unusual Hitler Grosser arrival, with sailors at right and helmeted General SS at left, men alternating facing in and out for security, as was standard. Such an arrangement might've saved John F. Kennedy's life at Dallas, where all the police faced but outward. (HHA.)

Sieg Heil!/Hail Victory! (HHA.)

A typical Hitlerian arrival by car at a German train station. Schaub sits on the right mid car jump seat, while Martin Bormann is at left rear and Schmundt at right rear. RSD chief Johann Rattenhuber is at the far right of the frame, outside the cars. (HHA.)

An excellent, prewar Hitlerian motorcade shot. (HHA.)

Another prewar Hitlerite motorcade view in license plate IA-103708: Hitler saluting, Kempka at the wheel, Schaub in the right mid car jump seat behind, and an RSD security car behind them all. (HHA.)

Another view of Hitler at the Nürnberg HJ stadium, with Kempka driving and Hess and von Schirach at the rear. (HJ.)

Another license plate IA-103708 view, with Hitler standing, Kempka driving, and Schaub in the mid section jump seat, the 770K Grosser followed by the standard RSD backup vehicle. (HHA.)

A Hitlerite arrival in Stüttgart, Württemberg, a Daimler-Benz company town, and site today of the company museum. The car is license plate IIA-19356, of Münich registry, with a pair of RSD cars behind. Hoffmann stands in the one at left, Leica camera in hand. (HHA.)

As I noted in 2006, "After 1933—and becoming Chancellor of Germany—Hitler found frenzied crowds wherever he went. People would wait hours just to have a glimpse of their new 'Führer.' Typically, security for the new Leader had to be tightened, as can be seen by the uniformed SS officer walking alongside Hitler's car [marked with the white X on SS black—who *may* be Baron Karl von Eberstein] and a plain clothes policeman just behind. In this photograph, SS Gen. Sepp Dietrich (standing behind Hitler) gestures to the lensman to move over as this photograph was taken." Note the car's wooden spoked wheels. (HHA.)

Hitler speaks at Stüttgart the same day. The banner at center reads *Ein Volk, Ein Reich, Ein Führer/One People, One Nation, One Leader*, a popular Nazi slogan of the period. (HHA.)

The same car and the same event, with SS Schaub sitting in the mid section jump seat and SA Brückner in the rear seating area. Note, too, the RAD buglers at right and wooden grandstands at rear, soon to be replaced with concrete ones that still stand today. (HHA.)

Nazi Party flag bearers hold their banners aloft as the *Führer's* car—license plate IIA-19357—arrives, with Schreck driving. The occasion is the September 1934 Nürnberg Party Congress. (HHA.)

Near Right: As I first wrote in 1969 of this outstanding photo, "In this scene—strongly reminiscent of Senator Robert F. Kennedy's 1968 Presidential campaign—Hitler reaches out to touch his avid supporters, who warmly welcome him to the 1934 Nürnberg Nazi Party Congress. At this point— Sept. 6, 1934—Hitler had been absolute dictator of Germany for a month and four days. The elimination of Röhm and his senior lieutenants on June 30th, the death of von Hindenburg on Aug. 2nd, and the swearing of an oath of personal allegiance to the Führer by the entire German Army swept all practical opposition to Hitler's rule out of the way."Thus, Hitler had much to be joyous about! Schreck drives, and Hitler's medals include the Iron Cross, First World War Wound Badge, and 1933 Nürnberg Rally Commemorative Badge. This is the only such shot of Hitler known to exist. Note the twin horns on either side, and the tri-pointed star at lower left on the hood. The smiling SS man in the car is unknown. (HHA.)

Two stills from Leni Riefenstahl's 1935 documentary film *Triumph of the Will* of the September 1934 Nürnberg Nazi Party Congress. The car is license plate IVB-27014. (Walter Frentz.)

Above: "Hitler in the leading car on *Konigsstrasse/King's Street*," downtown Nürnberg. (HHA.) Below:
Below: The same scene today. (Müller, *ATB.*)

A long view of the arrival of a Hitlerian motorcade arriving on Adolf Hitler Plaza for an annual September downtown Nürnberg Nazi Party Congress parade in downtown. The Grosser's windshield is in the down position as Hitler stands in front, peaked cap in his left hand. Schreck is at the wheel, while SA Brig. Gen. Wilhelm Brückner rides in back. (HHA.)

A trio of views of Hitler's car (license plate IIA-19357) on May Day 1934 on arrival at the Berlin Lustgarten with the *Führer's* Vice Chancellor—Franz von Papen— in the left rear seat with SA adjutant Wilhelm Brückner in the right. In the bottom right view, Berlin regular *Polizei/Police* walk alongside the Chancellor's vehicle ahead of his SS guards, an interesting combination. (Photos by Helmuth Kurth, Hermann Göring Albums, LC, Wash., DC.)

SS security men attempt to hold back the crowds as Hitler's car passes through a crowd. Children and others falling under the wheels were a real problem for these security officers. In the back seat at left is SA adjutant Brig. Gen. Brückner and Reich Press Chief Dr. Otto Dietrich in SS black at right (HHA.)

Another view of the same occasion, with Schreck seen driving. (HHA.)

A trio of photos of the same event and car, license plate IA-148760; the September 1938 Hitlerian arrival at the last Nürnberg Party Congress. In the middle shot, standing behind are (left) German Army C-in-C Col. Gen. Walther von Brauchitsch and right, Navy CO Adm. Dr. Erich Raeder. "The car was first shown at the February 1938 Berlin Auto Show, then returned to the factory for some additional work, before being presented to Hitler on his 49th birthday, Apr. 20, 1938. It was then used at Nürnberg," as I wrote in 1999. (HHA.)

Near Left: BDM girls scatter flowers on Hitler's parade route from the train station to the Old Reich Chancellery in Berlin on July 6, 1940, marking his return from the just concluded Western Campaign, a welcome unlike any since the ancient Roman Emperors. Note the car at right. (HHA.)

Below: During the *Führer's* triumphal return to Berlin on July 6, 1940, following the victorious French campaign, a car full of his happy aides ride in the same procession, from left to right: an SS chauffeur at the wheel with Martin Bormann (goggles on cap visor) beside him; jump seat (middle row) Naval aide Vice Adm. Karl-Jesko von Puttkamer, SS adjutant Max Wünsche, and *Luftwaffe* adjutant Col. Nikolaus von Below; back row, Göring's Air Force liaison officer with Hitler Gen. Karl Bodenschatz (left) and SS Escort Surgeon Dr. Karl Brandt, (right). (HHA.)

"Two million jubilant Berliners" welcome Hitler's motorcade before the war. His lead vehicle can be seen at upper left. (HHA.)

Not a Grosser, but Hitler's car pulling out of the gate of the Old Reich Chancellery in Berlin: Hitler saluting from up front with Kempka driving, a caped Hermann Göring sitting on the mid-car jump seat, an unknown *Luftwaffe* aide sitting behind him, and SA Gen. Wilhelm Brückner seated at right rear. Note the Berlin Regular Policeman giving a Nazi salute at center, on the opposite side of the car. Note also the two windows at the corner of the building at left, just above the top of the fence. This was formerly the apartment of the late Reich President von Hindenburg, and—starting in 1939—became Eva Braun's domicile when she stayed in Berlin. It was from one of these two windows that she shot the famous color footage of Hitler's Grosser pulling *into* the ORC courtyard on July 6, 1940, upon his return from the Western Front, that was most recently used in The History Channel's *Hitler's Bodyguard* series. (HHA.)

Hitler in Berlin during the war with all bulletproof windows in place. Note the spare wheel cover, nighttime driving lamp covers affixed, and *Führerstandarte* on the right wing. Note also the saluting trio of German Navy officers at right, across the street. (HHA.)

"Reich Chancellor Hitler arrives for a diplomatic reception in Berlin in 1939 in a 1938 Greater Mercedes," as I wrote in *Automotive News* in 1985. The Foreign Office man at left is unidentified. (JRA.)

Hitler on his way to speak before the German *Reichstag/Parliament* at the Berlin *Krollöper/Kroll* Opera House. Kempka drives, Krause sits on the jump seat mid car immediately behind his *Führer*, and—behind him at rear—Dr. Gœbbels (left) and Dr. Robert Ley. (right.)

As I wrote in 1985 in *Automotive News,* "Hitler enters the remilitarized Rhineland on March 28, 1936, and receives a bouquet from a small boy of the Hitler Youth at Cologne. At the wheel is Julius Schreck, who died less than two months after this picture was taken. Hitler wasn't involved in the auto accident." (HHA.)

Hitler's Grosser arrives at the front door of the Krollöper/Kroll Opera House in Berlin, the home of the Nazi *Reichstag* after the burning of the original building (now restored) on February 27, 1933. Hitler and Schreck are up front, an SS officer (left), and Hitler's Naval aide (right) are on the jump seats, and two unidentified men are in the rear. Sepp Dietrich salutes at the left, and Göring awaits at center to greet his *Führer.* (HHA.)

The *Führer's* motorcade has just driven through the Brandenburg Gate at rear between the two Nazi pylons with gilt swastikas on top. He stands in the lead Grosser on the evening of April 19, 1939, the night before his 50th birthday. The occasion is the opening of the East-West Axis built by architect Albert Speer as a birthday present for his *Führer.* (HHA.)

A prewar nighttime Hitler motorcade arrival in Berlin. (HHA.)

Hitler on the way to his 50th birthday parade in Berlin on April 20, 1939, in license plate IA-148485 on the *Unter den Linden/Under the Linden Trees.* Kempka drives, and an unknown SS man sits at rear. Note the motion picture cameraman on the roof of one of the follow up cars at center rear, and the pylons with gilt golden eagles flanking the roadway. The statue in the background is of Prussian King Frederick II the Great on horseback. According to *After the Battle,* "It was removed by the Communists in 1950, but 30 years later it was re-erected in its rightful place outside the Crown Prince's Palace." (HHA.)

April 20, 1939, on Hitler's 50th birthday, "Followed by the usual RSD security cars. According to Swedish author Jan Melin, this car—IA-148764, is 'Either the pre-series or first production run' of this particular model," as I first wrote in 1999. Note Hitler's car at far left, in front of the German Army band, and the reviewing stand just visible in the upper left hand corner. (HGA.)

The *Reichshauptstadt/Reich capital* "treats him to a reception never before seen in Berlin," prewar, riding in license plate IA-103708. (HHA.)

The Hitler car parade route down the *Unter den Linden* of April 20, 1939, as it looks today: "Now dual carriageways on either side have left the central strip a pedestrian area," noted *After the Battle*. (ATB.)

"Hitler's motorcade comes through the Brandenburg Gate" to kick off the Berlin Summer Olympic Games on August 1, 1936. Note the Olympic banners fluttering next to those of the swastika underneath the *Brandenburger Tor*. The car is license plate IA-148764. (HHA.)

From *Automotive News*, 1985: "Hitler's wrist is grabbed by a woman in the friendly crowd on the road between München and the *Landesgrenze/Provincial Border*, Apr. 17, 1936," another of my favorite views of this era. Note the ordinary people in the throng. The be-goggled SS man at right is Karl Wilhelm Krause. Hitler wears a leather motoring coat. (HHA.)

As I wrote in 1985 in *Automotive News*, "In this photo—taken Apr. 17, 1936—Hitler seems to be telling the friendly crowd he has had enough. Hitler frequently drove through the German countryside until throngs forced him to give up the practice. The men holding back the crowds wear garb typical of motorists of the period: goggles, leather caps, and overcoats." This was taken on the Eibsee, and the men are members of his SS Escort Detail. This is one of the author's favorite photos due to its spontaneity. (HHA.)

September 1937: the motorcade of Hitler and Mussolini passes through the Brandenburg Gate during the *Duce's* State Visit to Germany as a German Army honor guard stands at attention at left, its banner dipped, the commander's saber drawn. (JRA.)

"Arrival in Klagenfurt": the car is license plate IA-103708. (HHA)

"The creator of Greater Germany in his homeland; a triumphant drive through Linz," Austria, wrote Heinrich Hoffmann in *Hitler in His Homeland*. (HHA.)

Five views of Hoffmann's "Jubilant accord in German Vienna, in front of the Burg Theater." (Citadel or Castle, or Town Theater.) The *Führer's* vehicle is license plate IIA-19356, and that of the RSD escort car at right is IIA-44962. Kempka drives. The date is either April 8 or 9, 1938. The entire route was lined by troops of the elite SSLAH. The vote ratifying Germany's annexation of Austria was held on April 10th, when the *Anschluss/Union* was overwhelmingly approved by the Austrian people. (HHA.)

An interesting moment during one of Hitler's Spring 1938 motorcades in Austria, as Krause leaps up from his jump seat to intercept the child's teddy bear, fearing that it might contain a bomb, as driver Kempka looks on at left Such occurrences were the constant bane of Hitler's various bodyguard units. (HHA.)

"The Führer drives to City Hall," Vienna, Spring 1938. (HHA.)

"All Austria echoes again," 1938. The car is license plate IA-103708. Kempka drives and Krause is in the left mid-section jump seat, ever watchful. White-shirted Austrian Nazis hold back the crowd at right, and the caps of the soldiers at left are also Austrian. (HHA.)

"Hitler's motorcade drove to the City Hall, with the Burg Theater in the background across the Ring. These photos originally appeared in a special edition of the Nazi newspaper *The People's Observer* for Hitler's 50th birthday on Apr. 20, 1939." (HHA.)

Automotive News, 1985:"Hitler enters the Lithuanian port of Memel [on the Baltic Sea] on March 23, 1939, driven by Erich Kempa. Memel had been taken from Germany by the Versailles Treaty" of June 28, 1919."'This land remains German always,'" the banner read—until the Red Army arrived in 1945, that is. Kempka drives, and Krause is in his usual jump seat spot in license plate Iav-148764. The car is a W 150 open tourer. Hitler had arrived by ship, and Naval Marines line the street at right. This was eight days after he'd entered Prague in his G-4, and his last peaceful territorial acquisition before the German invasion of Poland on September 1, 1939. (HHA.)

The same date, event, and car: the *Führer* in Memel, as an RSD man walks alongside the vehicle at center and a German Army honor guard presents arms with fixed bayonets. (HHA.)

A wartime visit to a car factory at Steyr, Austria, in 1942. Hitler wears a light, white rain coat, and at his right is Austrian Gauleiter August Eigruber, hanged by the Allies after the war at Landsberg Prison as a convicted war criminal. Behind Hitler and to the left is Schaub, and at right Martin Bormann. Next to him is RSD chief Johann Rattenhuber. (HHA.)

Hitler in a Grosser at Steyr, Austria, during his 1942 visit. Kempka drives, and SS valet Heinz Linge stands just behind Hitler at left. Gauleiter August Eigruber is also seen, but obscured just behind Hitler at center. Note also that the wartime nightlight lamp covers are in place, as is the fog lamp at bottom center on the grill. (HHA.)

Hitler and Mussolini in the rear of a 770K Grosser Mercedes on the afternoon of July 20, 1944, the day of the abortive German Army bomb plot to kill the *Führer* at *FHQ Wolf's Lair*. This was one of the last public usages of the Grosser car line. Kempka drives, Julius Schaub sits in the front passenger seat, and the bulletproof windows are all in place. Bringing up the rear at right are SS valet Heinz Linge, running to keep up and carrying Hitler's black rain cape. Hitler's longtime chef Artur Kannenberg is seen at the left rear of the car, wearing a dark civilian suit and standing near the tree. Another, unknown vehicle—top up—can be seen at the right rear, behind Linge. The Grosser is pulling away from the railway platform at the nearby Görlitz station. License plate unknown. Note the lamp cover in place at the bottom center of the frame. (Previously unpublished photo from the Heinrich Hoffmann Albums, USNA, College Park, MD.)

Two previously unpublished views from a Heinrich Hoffmann contact sheet of Hitler leaving the Karlshof Hospital near *FHQ Wolf's Lair* at Rastenburg, East Prussia, following the bomb attempt on his life. Here, a slightly wounded Hitler shows himself to soldiers and nurses, and also received medical treatment himself. As he enters the Grosser Mercedes from the left rear passenger door, SS Escort Surgeon Dr. Karl Brandt gets in from the opposite side, and SS driver Kempka turns his head to watch. All the bulletproof windows are in place on this day of days. In the background, the many female nurses give Nazi salutes enthusiastically. In the partial frame at right, Hitler gives a casual Nazi salute with his *left* hand because his right was injured in the bomb blast. Martin Bormann sits next to him at rear, and Dr. Brandt sits on the left mid-car jump seat. (HHA.)

As I wrote in 1985 in *Automotive News*, "To refute rumors of his death after the bomb plot against him, a wounded Hitler [with cotton in his right ear—his eardrum was damaged)] salutes with his left hand, greeting soldiers and nurses at Karlshof Hospital. Martin Bormann is next to him. Bulletproof windows are" in place. Sitting in the mid-section left jump seat is SS Dr. Karl Brandt (1904-48), seen holding on to the bar in front of him with his left hand. Dr. Brandt was charged, tried, and convicted of war crimes against humanity for SS euthanasia killings of mentally ill Germans, as well as inhumane medical experiments on POWs during the war. In late 1944 he tried to displace Hitler's personal physician, Dr. Theodor Morell, in Hitler's confidence ,but failed, and was fired instead. His ultimate reward was the Allied hangman's noose at Landsberg Prison in Bavaria. (HHA.)

Another previously unpublished contact sheet view of a jovial Hitler (left) saluting with his left hand and with Nazi Party Secretary to the *Führer* SS *Reichsleiter/National Leader* Martin Bormann sitting at right next to him. SS Dr. Karl Brandt shifts leftward in the mid car jump seat and looks directly into the lens at center, as SS Gen. Julius Schaub sits in the right front passenger seat as Kempka drives—an interesting and unusual seating pattern for all of them except Kempka. Note, too, the RSD and other security men keeping watch outside the car, in between it and the throng of saluting nurses and soldiers. (HHA.)

6

The Survivors—1945 and Afterward

"My decisive experience with the Mercedes," recalled Adolf Hitler once, "was a collision... The other car was totally wrecked; on mine, only the bumpers and running board were damaged. It was then I decided to use only a Mercedes for the rest of my life."

Others would later think so, too. Indeed, after the war in 1945, a delegation of United States Senators rode in a captured U.S. Army star-emblazoned Mercedes-Benz W 150 open tourer from the Nazi dictator's former fleet. As noted by the late American author Stephen E. Ambrose in his book *Band of Brothers*, men of the 101st Airborne Division pushed one of Hitler's captured "luxury cars" off the side of a cliff to see if it would survive the crash, so well thought of were they; it didn't, alas.

A number of former "Hitler cars" continued to make news with their capture by the Allies in 1945 and, indeed, many decades later. Here is a review some of them.

Treasury to Exhibit Hitler, Göring Cars

That was the headline of a *New York Times* story that appeared in its Saturday, October 20, 1945, edition: "Wash., Oct. 19th—The personal automobiles of Adolf Hitler and Hermann Göring rolled through this city today in a freight car.

"Covered with protective grease, the two Mercedes-Benz arrived a short time later at a Rosslyn, VA freight station across the Potomac River, where they were unloaded, and taken to Ft. Myer.

"Brought to this country at the request of the (US) Treasury Department's War Finance Division—for use in the coming Victory Loan Drive—the cars will be cleaned, and then taken on a exhibition tour.

"The autos arrived at New York and were accompanied on their triumphant voyage to America's capital by Pvt. Joseph DeBois of Port Byron, NY, and PFC Emil Wortman of Omaha, NB, whose job was to see that souvenir hunters did not strip the prizes.

"Göring's low, sleek convertible coupe was unloaded with little difficulty, but Hitler's 19-foot-long, convertible sedan gave the men under Maj. R.M. Hood—post Ordnance officer of Ft. Myer—an unpleasant afternoon of jacking and towing, and the fact that the car weight was more than 10,000 pounds did not make it any easier.

According to late American World War II author Stephen E. Ambrose, "1ˢᵗ Sgt. Floyd Talbert on Hitler's staff car. Ordered to turn it over to the brass, Talbert first conducted an experiment to see if the windows really were bulletproof. He found that armor-piercing ammo would do the job. Next, he drained the water from the radiator. Only then did he turn it over to the regimental staff," from *Band of Brothers*, the book that spawned the epic History Channel TV series. (Talbert.)

"The cars are constructed of armor plate. Hitler's has 2 ½" bulletproof glass. Göring's bulletproof glass is only about an inch thick.

"The Treasury said the cars would be exhibited in as much of the country as can be covered during the Victory Loan drive, Oct. 29th–Dec. 8th. This is the tentative itinerary: Hitler's car—Pennsylvania, Ohio, Indiana, Illinois, and Iowa. Göring's: Washington, Massachusetts, Rhode Island, Connecticut, New York, Pennsylvania, Virginia, North Carolina, Tennessee, Arkansas, Maryland, West Virginia, Kentucky, and Missouri."

From the "Eagle's Nest" to the Champs Elysees
The following article appeared on December 2-3, 1945, in the French publication *Le Figaro*:

"Of massive lines, somewhat elegant, shining paint, numerous headlights, the hundreds of horses of Hitler is exhibited behind a vast glass enclosure at the Renault Exhibition Hall.

"This is not the automobile of propaganda photos in which one saw the Führer standing under the sun or in inclement weather 'heiling' the German people—palm outstretched, thumb at moustache level—but rather a comfortable, enclosed limousine furnished with the most up to date armor plating.

"It was discovered by our soldiers when they arrived at Berchtesgaden."

Hitler Car Fails to Draw Minimum Bid
This article appeared on January 12, 1982, in the Whittier, CA, *Daily News,* hometown of former U.S. President Richard M. Nixon:

"Phoenix, AZ (UPI)—Adolf Hitler's bulletproof Mercedes-Benz failed to draw a minimum $500,000 bid at auction, but a Texas car collector paid $240,000 for the Mercedes roadster that the Führer gave his mistress Eva Braun...Tom Barrett withdrew Hitler's parade car because the top bid was only $400,000.

"'I'll hold onto it until the time is right, the money is right, and the right person will appreciate it,' Barrett said. 'That's the most important—the person who will appreciate it as a historical car.'

"...About 1,000 cars were sold at the auction, claimed to be the largest of its type in the world, for 'Close to $10 million,' according to a spokesman."

The Fate of W 24 Experimental Car License Plate IA-103708
What happened to the W 24 Experimental Car license plate IA-103708?

It is part of the City of Lyon (France) Museum Henri Malartre Collection of Automobiles, Cycles, and Motors, according to a letter written to the author by its Director, B. Vaireaux, on December 17, 2002.

The brochure noted, "During the Second World War, Mercedes-Benz AG was commissioned to prepare a special car, incorporating the required safeguards and specifications for the Leader of the Third Reich, Adolf Hitler.

"The car chosen was the already well known 7.7 liter Grand Mercedes, which had already been in production since 1938. Amongst the substantial changes noticed from the car at the Rochetaillee-sur-Saone (Lyon) Museum a few years ago were two personal Führer banners, flown one on each side of the bonnet (hood), bulletproof windscreen and all other windows; apart from the two main headlamps, three additional front spot lamps and two hand spot lamps operated from the side of the windscreen.

"The entire rear part of the body had a built in armor protection shield. Technical items: eight cylinders, 95mm bore, 135mm stroke, 7655cmc total cubic capacity, 2000 tours/minute normal peak 100km/ph., 3200 tours/minute maximum peak at maximum speed 155CV no compression power break (170km/ph.), 230 CV compressed; compression (with the fuel available at that time) 1:600; speeds five onward, one backward; proportion gearbox 1:3, 65:2,25; : 1,48; :1 r. :3,65; connection axle motor 1:4, 11; total connection in the maximum speed 1:2,96; on wheels suspension two turning arms per side, with helicoidal springs; rear wheel suspension parallel axle with helicoidal springs; break oil dynamic, assisted by a vacuum help apparatus; wheelbase 3380mm; track on 1600 mm, rear 1650mm.

"Height from ground 200mm. Diameter of turning 15m. Total length 6000mm. Total width 2070mm. Total height 1800mm. Weight 3600 kg. Tires 8, 25" X 17."

According to the brochure, the car was ridden in by Hitler, Benito Mussolini, Eva Braun Hitler, Karl Wilhelm Krause, Wilhelm Brückner, Erich Kempka, and French soldiers after the war, among others.

Then and Now: Adolf Hitler's Mercedes-Benz Canadian War Museum Brochure
"The US 101st Airborne Division confiscated the Mercedes-Benz model 770 W 150 car at the end of the war in Europe.

"However, after further research in 1980 (!), it was found that this information [denoting the Hitler car as a *Göring* car instead] was incorrect, and that the car was the Mercedes that Hitler drove in his heyday.

"The automobile was built in 1940, and bears the serial # 429334 on the still existing license plate. This has been confirmed by order file # 366986 in the Daimler-Benz Archives. On July 8, 1940—two days after Hitler triumphantly returned to Berlin from the French campaign—the stately Mercedes was driven to Berlin under its own steam, and handed over to the Führer's aide-de-camp at the New Reich Chancellery's car pool.

"A few days later—on July 19th—Hitler was filmed in this car with the Police (license) # 148697 in a newsreel. Hitler used this vehicle several times in the course of the next three years.

"Towards the end of April 1945, the US 20th Armored Division under Maj. Gen. Orlando Ward took part in the fighting in Southern Germany. The division fought near München, and marched towards Salzburg, Austria. It was on May 4th or 5th when Joe Azara—a lance corporal from the Ordnance unit—discovered a heavy car fastened down to an open goods wagon on a sidetrack near Laufen.

"He came under fire as he tried to approach, but succeeded in driving the riflemen away, and with the help of some fellow soldiers, got the car on the road, found it drivable, and set off.

"Shortly afterward, however, the car came to a stop due to engine damage. The oil in the engine was too light, causing the engine to overheat. The connecting rod was also broken.

"Lance Cpl. Azara, however, was up to the task. American newspapers reported that he 'acquired' an engine from the same model car constructed in 1944, which belonged to the 101st Airborne Division.

"In May 1945, the 20th Armored Division's magazine reported that the car was to be transported to Berchtesgaden. The 20th Armored Division left Europe in late July 1945, and arrived in New York harbor on Aug. 6th.

"Two days later, the Mercedes was unloaded at Castle Island harbor from the ship *George Shiras*. The same day, the Boston *Globe* printed an illustrated article with the misleading headline *Göring's Mercedes is bulletproof*. The article retold the Göring legend, which accompanied the car for the next 35 years as it crisscrossed America and Canada.

"It was only in 1982—when Ludwig Kosche published his research in the journal *After the Battle* #35 that the story was refuted. This car was used not by Göring, but by Hitler himself almost without interruption until 1943.

"The Mercedes was exhibited all over America, and later stored from 1947-56. It was then auctioned in 1956 to a car dealer from Toronto, who sold it to the collector H.J. O'Connell. After extensive restoration, the automobile was sold to Claude Pratte, who placed it at the disposal of the Canadian War Museum.

"The Mercedes has been on exhibit there since 1971."

From *After the Battle* #119, 2003

"...We received a letter from Irving Cohen of Northridge, CA, who captured another large car said to have been Göring's." Mr. Cohen wrote that, because of boobytrapped doors, "I was undecided about opening the garage doors. I had my rifle and bayonet, so curiosity got the best of me, and I proceeded to open one door very slowly...I noticed a car in the garage.

"The lady told me it was Hermann Göring's. The car had two spare tires bolted on the back, one on the left front fender, one on the right front fender, and the cloth top was still up, and bolted to the front windshield...

"I was always a car buff, and so-so mechanic in civilian life....I finally opened the car door and pushed the leather type seat to the floor...I then got bold and sat on the seat! The dashboard had a factory made switch for the ignition. I turned the key on and checked the gas, it had ¾ tank full!

"I then proceeded to step on the spring-type starter lever next to the brake pedal. It started very easy, and thank God it was not boobytrapped...I put the shift lever in reverse, and slowly backed the car out of the garage. I knew better not to drive on the open road because the MPs would grab me, so I kept the car, driving every day on the grassy fields, until after four or five days it ran out of gas!

"'No one in my battery knew that I had the car, and I never told anyone because of the risk of being court-martialed.'

"One wonders what happened to the Mercedes after Pvt. Cohen abandoned it and, even more so, if it survives today."

Other Vintage Nazi Mercs

One was examined at the British Ministry of Supply's Wheeled Vehicle Experimental Establishment at Chertsey in 1946, and another found its way to the Montagu Motor Museum at Beaulieu, Hampshire, England.

License plate WL-461462 in that same year was exhibited as a fundraising attraction in the showroom of the Bedfordshire Autocar Company Ltd. Ford dealership in England in The Broadway at Bedford. Money was thus raised for the Soldiers, Sailors, and Airmens' Families Association, which explained that British soldiers had fired the bullets at the windshield and side windows.

On May 5, 1971, an ex-RSD car was finally and positively identified when the British magazine *Motor* published the fact that its license plate WL-461462 had been found in a green canvas bag, also so marked. It developed that the Royal Air Force had seized the car in 1945 at Amelinghausen, on Luneberg Heath, near where German Grand Adm. Karl Dönitz had the last Nazi Reich Government at Flensburg.

This raises an intriguing question. In his 1970 *Inside the Third Reich: Memoirs*, Albert Speer noted of the comic operetta government established there, "Even one of Hitler's big Mercedes limousines had found its way to Flensburg and served to convey Dönitz to his home, all of 500 yards from the offices of the government."

Could this be the car that Speer saw? We don't know for sure. In the early 1970s, Britisher E. Black restored Grosser WL-461462, and in the 1980s it sported a new convertible top. It had been auctioned in the U.S. on July 6, 1974, as pictured in the then Baltimore newspaper *The Evening Sun*, for which the current author used to write freelance articles until the paper's demise.

The Final Word: *After the Battle*

"...Joe Azara died in 1967...Iav48697 was subsequently prepared for the use of Brig. Gen. Cornelius M. Daly (who died in 1974), commanding Combat Command A of the 20th Armored Division. It was repainted in olive drab and given the markings of a captured vehicle and the single star befitting Gen. Daly's rank."

Here I believe that the British author of this piece is himself wrong. Having been a U.S. Army infantryman during 1965-67 in the Vietnam War era, I can attest that U.S. Army vehicles *all* had the white star, and that it had and has nothing to do with any general officer's rank, being instead a symbol of the entire force, not of any one person.

"His superior—Maj. Gen. Orlando Ward—is also reported to have availed himself of the services of this eminent war trophy. In Europe the driver was Sgt. Edwin J. Lasko (then of Centerville, MI), while late, in the States...Cpl. James A. Pendas drove it as well, and found that handling it was as easy 'as pie.'

"...The Boston *Daily Globe*...headlined its article *Göring's Auto Bulletproof to Protect Fat Marshal's Hide*" in a little bit of wartime journalistic hyperbole. "Of the two photographs included in the newspaper's report, the first was republished by *Newsweek* on Aug. 20, 1945...

"It is not known whether Iav148697 went with the division to Camp Cooke, CA, or if it was sent directly to the US Army Ordnance Museum at Aberdeen Proving Ground near Baltimore in Maryland....and given a new registration in the German style: W-169290...

"The car went on the bond tour accompanied by Sgts. Azara and Lasko, Cpl. Pendas, as well as Lt. John J. Cole. Throughout the tour, it was advertised as 'Göring's car.'...In April 1946...doubts had arisen as to whether it really had been one of Göring's cars...

"During 1947, the car was transferred to the Property Disposal Office, which apparently kept it in storage for nearly a decade." The car was then auctioned, and arrived at Toronto on December 19, 1956. "It was in poor condition." Transferred to Montreal, the car had been restored during 1957.

"Finally, his information led [Toronto car dealer R.J.] Rumble to think that the US 101st Airborne Division had captured the car he was trying to restore.

"Maj. Gen. Maxwell D. Taylor's 101st Airborne had, in fact, taken over several Mercedes-Benz cars when it occupied the Obersalzberg and The Berghof complex. In the division's history *Rendezvous with Destiny,* Leonard Rapport speaks of three such cars, though the real number may have been closer to five.

"At the request of the US Treasury Department, the division sent two of these captured vehicles to the United States....Thus, all three Mercedes-Benz cars which had been shipped to the US in the summer and autumn of 1945 were evidently mixed up, and a decade later, R.J. Rumble became one more victim of this confusion. He was not the last one..."

After 1980, "All the evidence flatly contradicts the legend that the armored Grosser Mercedes in the Canadian War Museum (at Ottawa) was 'Göring's staff car.' It is, in fact, one of the cars which Hitler used during the heyday of his devastating career, and it was not the 101st Airborne which captured it, but Sgt. Joe Azara of the 20*th* Armored, 'the luckiest and best division in the whole damn Army.'"

According to Jan Melin, "Two armored Grosser Mercedes Offener Tourenwagen/Open Touring Cars (chassis numbers 150006/0024 and 15000625) were awaiting delivery at the works when destroyed during the March 2, 1944 air raid." (DBM.)

"Göring's car—Charles Butler, June 22, 1945," on the fourth anniversary of the German invasion of the USSR. The man is an American Army captain, and the car is a Pullman. Note the width of the door! (Frank Quigley.)

Another grosser in Allied hands, 1945. (LC.)

According to the U.S. Army Signal Corps' photo caption, "Heinrich Himmler's car goes into a GI motor pool. The 155 hp Mercedes-Benz of the late Nazi Gestapo chief has been converted to GI use at the Bremen port command headquarters motor pool. Trying the driver's seat for size is the motor pool dispatcher, Staff Sgt. Joseph B. McCracken, Jonesboro, TN, while assistant dispatcher Cpl. Hazel Mulligan, Middleport, NY, examines the 1 ½"-thick window glass. Bremen, Germany, Oct. 18, 1945." Note also the door thickness! (USNA.)

Far Left: A good postwar view of steering wheel, dashboard, and windshield. (LC.)

Near Left: License plate HG 12 742 in postwar British captivity. As I wrote in 2006, "A number of Grossers and G-4s *did* survive the Second World War—exactly how many of each is still a question mark, however. Perhaps the definitive answer to this question may never be known." The car shown here was originally license plate WL-461462 (L being the designation for *Luftwaffe*) in England after the war, on February 25, 1946, in London. The car is a 770K W 150 Grosser Mercedes, here showing its British license HG 122 42. The driver is unknown. Note the apparent attempts to shatter the windshield and bulletproof side windows, which failed. (LC.)

An unknown Grosser Mercedes used with my October 30, 1985, article in *Automotive News' Centennial Celebration of the Car Special Issue.* In 1982 this car—with *Führerstandarte* in place and rear bulletproof shield up and windows in place—was auctioned at Phoenix, AZ, with the minimum bid set at $ 500,000. (LC.)

J. T. TERRY BRUNE
P. O. BOX 207, THE GREEN
IRVINGTON, VA 22480

Mr. Blaine Taylor
Combined Publishing
Conshohocken, PA   18 Oct 2001

Dear Mr. Taylor
    I thought you might be interested in the enclosed photograph taken by my Father. Father was a Captain with the HQ Co. of the XVIII Airborne Corps and accompanied some intelligence officers to Berchtesgaden. He remembered two large Benz staff cars, both in running order, which were the object of much curiosity. I remember him telling me that at some point a group of GI's took one of the cars out for a drive and were fired on by a British patrol. An American LT was injured seriously, if not fatally, which required a hush-up.
    In Father's picture the soldiers appear to be 101st Airborne, which was under XVIII Corps at that time, and he mentioned that Gen. Taylor had wanted one of the cars for his own use. The mark on the left rear fender looks suspiciously like a bullet hole.
    One thing I noticed was that the spare tire covers are metal. In your book this is not common.
    I hope this is of some interest to you, I recently read " Band of Brothers" by Stephen Ambrose, and was horrified by the stories concerning the Benz autos they wrecked
    Sincerely yours

    Terry Brune

A Grosser Mercedes Type W 150 open tourer parade car captured by the U.S. Army on the Obersalzberg in May 1945. The unit was E Company of the 506th Regiment of the 101st Airborne Division, which landed at Normandy on D-Day, June 6, 1944, and then fought its way across Western Europe to The Berghof. After the war, the veterans told the late author Stephen E. Ambrose of the "fabulous cars" they found there. (J.T. Terry Brune, Irvington, VA.)

Letter to the author of October 18, 2001, concerning the car shown in the previous picture. (J.T. Terry Brune, Irvington, VA.)

According to *After the Battle,* "Berlin-Tempelhof, Aug. 24, 1939. Hitler arrives less than 24 hours after the signing of the Nazi-Soviet Non-Aggression Pact; 28 years later, this was the car which served as a model for restoring IAv148698 seen in the Canadian War Museum in 1980." The photo shows license plate IA-148485 with driver Kempka and Hitler in front, von Below on the right mid car jump seat, and Schaub in the right rear seat. (HHA.)

As I wrote in my 2006 work *Apex of Glory,* "The captured 770 Pullman Limousine on display at Brussels during 1946. According to the French publication *Le Figaro* of December 1945, 'The car was given by Gen. Jacques Le Clerc to Gen. Charles de Gaulle, and he has allowed *Victoire/Victory,* the national solidarity organization of soldiers (a veterans group) to begin exhibiting the car for profit.' Pullman Limousines of this type were a variant of the second series of Grosser Mercedes-Benz built by Daimler-Benz AG from 1938-42. This example was one, and probably the last, of only four closed cars delivered to Hitler's Adjutancy. The Daimler-Benz Commissions Book assigned this chassis with coach number 200787 and engine number 15000610005. The completed car was delivered to Münich on Feb. 2, 1943," the day that the German 6th Army surrendered to the Red Army at Stalingrad. "By 1945, the car had been left at The Berghof, and this is when it was removed by the French 2nd Armored Division under Gen. Le Clerc. The car was placed on exhibition in Paris in November 1945, then was exhibited in Brussels during 1946, then Geneva in May 1947, before being shipped to the USA." (LC.)

The same car photographed at Trostberg, June 1945. According to *After the Battle,* "At this stage, the car lacked both the original registration number and any captured markings." (Cpl. James A. Pendas.)

"One of Hitler's Mercedes-Benz cars on display at the Imperial Palace Casino at Las Vegas. Ludwig Kosche, the former Librarian of the Canadian War Museum, who authored the *After the Battle* story on Hitler's cars in Issue 35, passed away on May 17, 2000." License plate IAv-148461. (Imperial Palace, Las Vegas.)

Added *After the Battle*, "This is the first photograph to show—under magnification—the damage to the windscreen as well as the scratch on the top center of the dashboard which, 35 years later, are still to be seen on the car. Note that the sun visors have disappeared. Sgt. Azara is behind the steering wheel, with Cpl. Pendas in the passenger seat." (Cpl. James A. Pendas.)

As I wrote in 2006 in *Apex of Glory*, "A photograph of a captured Mercedes-Benz 770K staff car, being used by the US Army Military Police during 1945." (USNA.)

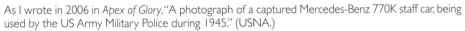

U.S. Army Sgt. T3 Joe Azara at the steering wheel of the car he captured at Laufen, 16 kilometers north of Salzburg, Austria, in a photo taken sometime during May-June 1945 by Cpl. James A. Pendas. (*ATB.*)

As I wrote in 2006 in *Apex of Glory*, "Sgt. Joseph Azara of the US Army 20th Armored Division props himself up against one of Hitler's Mercedes-Benz Type 770K. The photograph was taken at Berchtesgaden on May 12, 1945. The hole in the window was made by a US .50 caliber bullet." In addition to shooting at the window—noted the late author Stephen E. Ambrose in *Band of Brothers*—the men drained all the water from the Grosser's radiator! The object was to see if the massive automobile would run without it! Predictably, the car's engine burned out on the road up to the Eagle's Nest on the Kehlstein Mountain. (U.S. Army Signal Corps, USNA.)

Stated *After the Battle*, "The photograph released in October 1945 of the two '101st Airborne' Mercedes. The original captions reads: 'Touring the United States for the 8th Victory Loan Drive are these two automobiles belonging to *Reichsführer (sic)* Adolf Hitler and Marshal Hermann Göring. Driven by men of the 101st Airborne Division who found the vehicles at Berchtesgaden, Germany, Göring's car (left) is powered with an 180hp motor, while Hitler's automobile (right) has 160hp. Both are custom built 1943 Mercedes-Benz models and equipped with ½-inch armor plate steel and 2" bulletproof glass. Ft. Myer, VA, October 1945.' The reversal probably owes its origin to the fact that, to the driver, the Göring sports car is on the left." To make this simpler, Hitler's Grosser is the car at left and Göring's sports roadster that on the right, both with U.S. Army markings on the fenders. (U.S. Army Signal Corps, USNA.)

Continued *After the Battle*, "The captor of IAv148697 and his friends in a relaxed mood. From left to right, Cpl. T5 James A. Pendas, Sgt. T3 Joe Azara, 1st Lt. John J. Cole, and Sgt. Edwin J. Lasko." (Cpl. James A. Pendas.)

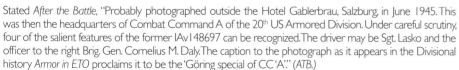

Stated *After the Battle*, "Probably photographed outside the Hotel Gablerbrau, Salzburg, in June 1945. This was then the headquarters of Combat Command A of the 20th US Armored Division. Under careful scrutiny, four of the salient features of the former IAv148697 can be recognized. The driver may be Sgt. Lasko and the officer to the right Brig. Gen. Cornelius M. Daly. The caption to the photograph as it appears in the Divisional history *Armor in ETO* proclaims it to be the 'Göring special of CC 'A'.'" (ATB.)

Noted *After the Battle*, "When the engine of what was then erroneously labeled 'Göring's car' broke down, Sgt. Azara removed the one from the Mercedes-Benz (Order # 399902) pictured at Trostberg, some 40 kilometers northwest of Salzburg." (Cpl. James A. Pendas.)

From the brochure accompanying the *Adolf Hitler Mercedes-Benz:* "In 1970, the Canadian War Museum bought a historical armored Mercedes-Benz model 770 W 150. Since 1945, this automobile has generally been ascribed to Hermann Göring. It was thought that the car was assigned to him from Hitler's Headquarters." Later, Museum Librarian Ludwig Kosche wrote a detailed article proving that the car was not Göring's but, indeed, one of the *Führer's* own. Note the white U.S. Army star on the side. (U.S. Army Signal Corps, USNA.)

The same car being unloaded in Boston in 1945 after having been used as a U.S. Army staff car. Described as "Marshal Göring's car" in the press, Hitler's State Coach is here being unloaded from Troopship *George Shiras*. (U.S. Army Signal Corps, USNA.)

Stated *After the Battle*, "Advertisement dated Nov. 12, 1945—the picture probably having been taken in September/October after the car had been repainted. Note the huge red spotlight which has replaced the American pattern siren, and the crude, handwritten registration number." The current author has resided at Towson, MD, near this armory for the past two decades! (*ATB.*)

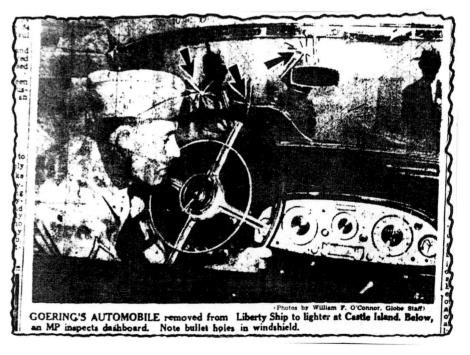

A newspaper clipping from the Boston *Daily Globe* of August 8, 1945, article "with the damage caused to the windscreen arrowed," according to *After the Battle*. (Wm. F. O'Connor, *Globe* staff.)

Continued *After the Battle*, "Photograph datelined Wash., DC, Apr. 10, 1946 when the car was displayed at the Barry-Pate Motor Company, Inc. on Connecticut Avenue in support of a recruiting drive." The original captions do not mention the 20th Armored Division as having captured the vehicle. (U.S. Army Signal Corps, USNA.)

Continues *After the Battle*, "Master Sgt. E. Chones and Staff Sgt. E.C. Shipley inspect the instrument panel (dashboard)—the scratch at the top is clearly visible, as is the damage to the windscreen. The reading on the odometer is on the point of showing 13,900 kilometers as reported in the Boston *Daily Globe* article the previous year." (U.S. Army Signal Corps.)

Another view of the same event with the following official caption: "Capt. W.A. Blasé (left), Master Sgt. E. Chones (center), and Staff Sgt. E.C. Shipley stand alongside Hermann Göring's personal car (sic) on display in the window of Barry-Pate Motor Co., Inc., on Connecticut Ave., Wash. DC." (U.S. Army Signal Corps, USNA.)

"Toronto, Dec. 19, 1956: the car on its arrival—somewhat despoiled." (R.J. Rumble/*ATB.*)

"R.J. Rumble at the wheel of Herbert O'Connell's prize acquisition." (R.J. Rumble/*ATB.*)

"After its restoration—but not quite the same any longer." Note new license plate: 1052-M. (R.J. Rumble/*ATB.*)

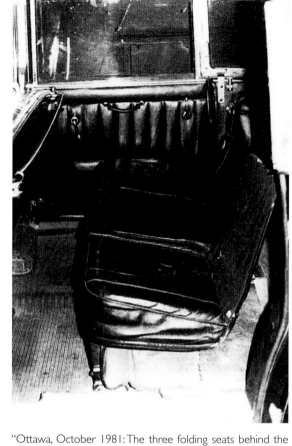

"IAv148607 in Montreal in 1958." (*ATB.*)

The Hitler Grosser as it appeared in 1970 at the Canadian War Museum. Note that the rear protection shield is in its raised position at right rear. (*ATB.*)

"Ottawa, October 1981: The three folding seats behind the front seats—characteristic of the cars which Hitler used," i.e., jump seats. (*ATB.*)

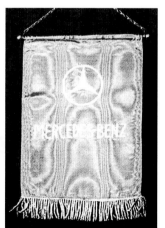

"In 1970 at the *Man and His World* exhibition. At last billed as "Hitler's Car," it would've been more accurate to have stated: 'One of Hitler's cars.'" (W. Schleich and City of Montreal/*ATB.*)

"Cpl. Pendas found this pennant in the car and kept it for more than 35 years." It is a small Mercedes-Benz flag with three-pointed star emblem. (Cpl. James A. Pendas.)

"The damage which still exists on the front passenger window"—where Hitler used to sit. Also, note the rich upholstered interior. *(ATB.)*

"The genuine registration (license) plate mounted in the rear moulding below the boot (hood). The white border all round seems to be indicative of the plate having been mounted initially in the frame in front of the radiator." *(ATB.)*

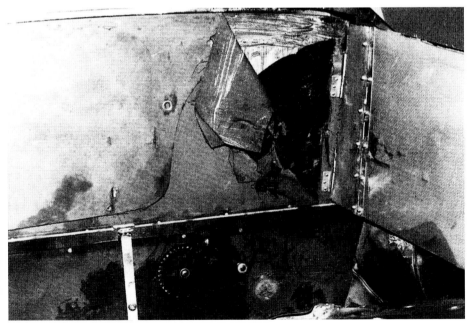

"Some of the bullet holes in the armor plate at the rear are still noticeable close to the hinges on the right. At the bottom is the winder for raising the plate," at the rear of the car to protect Hitler from weaponry fire. *(ATB.)*

The car put at auction at Phoenix, AZ, that failed to garner the opening bid of $500,000. Note the wartime lamp cover at right. (LC.)

Into the future: a model of Hitler's 770K Grosser Mercedes-Benz in its Nürnberg Nazi Party Congress reviewing stand mode, as sold by PzG, Inc. (PzG, Inc.)

The end for Mercedes-Benz passengers Adolf and Eva Braun Hitler, who committed suicide on April 30, 1945. Their bodies were doused with gasoline from Kempka's NRC garage and burned. Here—that summer—an American Army GI looks down, as two Red Army men watch, into the famous shallow ditch, holding one of the World War II jerry cans that, oddly, never became a souvenir hunter's dream. What happened to them? Like much else about this period in history, we don't know: a fitting place to close. (U.S. Army Signal Corps, USNA.)

Four Historic—But Little Known!—Auto Accidents

The Hitler Car Accident

Despite Hitler's later protests that he had traveled hundreds of thousands of miles in cars without an accident, there was at least one such happening, as noted by Wegener in his 1985 work, *Hitler: Memoirs of a Confidante*, following an inspection tour of the future Nürnberg Party Rally grounds.

"In silence, we got back in the car for the return drive...Hitler to the right in front; behind him Hess and myself, and on the left—behind the driver—Schaub and Hoffmann... As we were about to cross the wide avenue in the southeast of the city that led to the center from the stadium—a crossing that widened into a small, triangular, open space—from the right a monster of a truck, hauling an equally overpowering trailer, came rushing ahead at a fairly rapid rate, only 10 or 15 kilometers away from us.

"We ourselves had slowed down to a speed of about 20 kilometers. Our driver at first stepped on the accelerator, and if he had only driven on, nothing at all would've happened. But—the devil knows why!—he braked abruptly in an effort to let the truck pass.

"Its driver, however—we subsequently learned that he did not even have a license, while the man who was the nominal operator sat next to him—though he braked as well, at the same time stepped on the gas, and while the real driver grabbed the wheel to rectify the situation, turned left, that is, straight at us, assuming that we would simply drive on. And so, this monster of a vehicle came rushing at our almost immobile car!

"I can still see the large letters 'Magirus' over me as the powerful radiator pushed its way over our car body, pressing Hitler, Hess, and myself to the left inside the car. Then the truck's frame and springs must've taken hold of our Mercedes and shoved it diagonally across the open triangle, a distance of about 20 meters, as far as the street corner, only to come to a stop at last at the instant when our left wheels were already touching the curb.

"Only a short stretch more, and the left wheels would've broken, and the monster would've run over the crushed car and passengers. After a few moments, the truck—with a terrible grinding of the motor, which was on top of us, reversed for a few meters and pulled its projecting radiator off of us.

"We could sit up again. Hitler, Hess, and I came away with several scratches on our faces, and contusions on our right shoulders. Except for that, it seemed we had not sustained any injuries. The others had suffered no more than a fright.

Münich policeman directing street traffic. (HHA.)

213

"Hitler was the first to regain his voice: 'Everyone still alive?' When I called out my assurance, he said, 'In fact, nothing could've happened to us! We have not yet completed our task.' Hoffmann whispered to me, 'Just the same, by a hair, it would've been the end of us.'

"We left the others and the car at the scene of the accident, since the police had to finish their report. Then Hitler, Hess, Schaub, and I took a taxi back to the hotel...The other car was not in working order, and Hess therefore had to stop at the Mercedes repair works."

Otto Wegener was almost executed during the June 30, 1934, Blood Purge, served in and survived World War II, and died at age 83 in 1971.

The Churchill Auto Accident, December 11, 1931

On December 11, 1931, British author Winston Churchill (1874-1965) and his wife Clementine were staying at New York City's famed Waldorf-Astoria Hotel, where they were preparing for a 40-city speaking tour in the United States on his books.

He received a phone call from American-Jewish financier Bernard Baruch to visit him at his nearby apartment, and so took a cab there. When Churchill thought that he saw the correct address, he told the cab driver to stop, got out, and started to cross the street—without looking both ways.

An unemployed Italian-American truck driver struck him down at 30 mph in his car, and Churchill lay in pain on Fifth Avenue for some time. Taken to New York's Lennox Hill Hospital for eight days, Clementine cabled their son Randolph that his father had "Head scalp wound severe...This terrible physical injury."

Nevertheless Winnie rebounded, telling his editor in London that he was, "Preparing two articles...upon how it seems to be run over by a motorcar." The car's driver attended Churchill's first lecture as his guest in Brooklyn, NY, on January 28, 1932.

It's interesting to speculate what might have happened had WSC been killed or incapacitated in this accident, and how the history of the world might have been changed thereby.

Most likely, Churchill would be recalled today—if at all!—as a discredited figure from World War I who'd failed at Gallipoli, opposed both Irish and Indian rights to home rule afterward (as well as women's right to vote), and thus ended his career as a successful author of English and American history—but no more.

As it was, Churchill went on to the great challenge of facing Hitler in 1940. He was, however, exactly what Hitler always said that he was: a hopeless drunk.

The Prewar Göring Car Accident

The following was found in the 1972 memoirs of the late Frau/Mrs. Emmy Sonnemann Göring, *My Life with Göring*:

"We were involved in a serious motor accident. We were driving rather fast up a mountain road when—just before the summit—we found ourselves face to face with a little car which was trying to pass an omnibus. Hermann braked hard, but crashed into the car. It was only slightly damaged, but our wheels were torn off, Hermann just got the steering wheel in his ribs, and was bleeding from both his mouth and nose.

"My head had crashed through the windscreen. Luckily, just before leaving Münich, I had had a tooth out. I had a swollen cheek, and I had wrapped my face with a thick scarf. It was thanks to the scarf that I did not have my face cut.

"Hermann's staff car—which accompanied us—took us first to the hospital at Rosenheim, and then to Obersalzberg. Hermann had two ribs broken and his nose was injured. I had received a windshield wiper in one eye, and had a good gash on my scalp. As a result, we had to stay several days at Obersalzberg instead of going on next day to Hermann's chalet, which was situated 2,000 meters higher.

"I had been somewhat alarmed at the idea of going there because my sciatica prevented me from walking very long. On the eve of my departure, I said to Gustav Grundgens, 'If only something could happen to enable me to avoid going up to the chalet!'

"Even to this day, I still have very unpleasant dreams about the accident."

The Wilhelm Brückner Automobile Accident

From Frau Göring as well:

"Herr Brückner was involved in an accident and seriously injured in the head. The other occupants of the car were also injured. Hermann and I put Brückner in our own car and drove him to Trauenstein, where he was operated on by SS Dr. Karl Brandt, a famous surgeon who happened to be with us."

"During the whole time the operation lasted—which was a good hour—Adolf Hitler walked up and down with me outside the hospital. He had tears in his eyes. 'My good Brückner!' said he. 'God grant that he will be all right again!' What a different man that was from the one who only a few days previously had answered me so coldly and heartlessly about the Jewish question."

More details on this incident were in the excellent 2007 biography by German author Ulf Schmidt entitled, *Karl Brandt: The Nazi Doctor/Medicine and Power in the Third Reich*: "On Aug. 15, 1933—while Hitler was spending a brief holiday at the Berghof/ Mountain Court—his adjutant Wilhelm Brückner, traveling behind Hitler, lost control of his car and drove into a ditch.

"Coming from Berchtesgaden, the entourage was on its way back to the Berghof when the accident happened near Reit im Winkel. Brückner suffered multiple serious injuries, including a fractured skull, a broken leg, and an eye injury. Hitler's half-sister—Angela Raubal—and her two female friends only suffered minor injuries directly to their faces.

"The car behind Brückner was driven by a young surgeon: Karl Brandt. His fiancée— Anni Rehborn—had been personally acquainted with Hitler since the mid-1920s. They were on holiday near Berchtesgaden, and spent their time in close proximity to the newly elected (sic) Chancellor [he was, in fact, appointed]...They had been invited to lunch with Hitler and his party at a hotel in Berchtesgaden when the accident occurred.

"Dr. Brandt immediately provided first aid and drove Brückner and one of the women to the nearest hospital in Traunstein. Clearly excited by their visitors, the hospital staff readily assisted Brandt while he operated on Brückner's fractured skull and removed one of his badly injured eyes.

"Sacrificing his holidays—and neglecting his professional duties—Dr. Brandt spent the next six weeks at Brückner's bedside until his condition had clearly improved. After the war, Brandt assigned an air of destiny to the incident, mystifying the circumstance which had brought him to Hitler's attention."

Indeed, for the next decade, Dr. Brandt served as the Führer's official Escort Physician on most of his many motorcades and travels, and was later appointed Reich Commissioner for Health and Sanitation, being hanged by the Allies after the war as a convicted criminal.

The *Führer* (center) waits in a relaxed mood wearing his famous velour hat as his plane is readied for takeoff at a German airport. SA Adjutant Wilhelm Brückner is directly behind him, and SS Dr. Karl Brandt listens as Brückner talks with two other Nazi officials. The man with the beard is the Propaganda Ministry's Karl Hanke, later *Gauleiter/Regional Leader* of Breslau, in Silesia. Recalled one German in 1973, "We crowded around the car. He had gotten out, and had a newspaper under his arm. He was wearing that slouch hat of his. And then—it's funny to say this today, but I remember it well—and then it seemed to me, because I stood right next to him, that he farted. You could smell it, couldn't you? In later years—when he became more and more famous, I always used to think of that." (HHA.)

German Reich Chancellor Hitler (center) examines the "Saxonette" wheel on October 5, 1938, at a prewar auto show. (HHA.)

In September 1930, the *Führer* (center) is seen—bouquet of flowers in hand from an admirer—about to enter a Mercedes Pullman Saloon car, following the political trial of the "Ulm lieutenants," young Nazi Army supporters of his. Behind him is Otto Wegener, SA Chief of Staff just before Ernst Röhm's return from Bolivia to resume his former post. Wegener was then the head of the Economic Policy Section of the Nazi Party. (HHA.)

Wartime anti-bombing camouflage netting over a Berlin street near the famed Brandenburg Gate, late in 1939. These were "Strips of brown and green burlap in netting that simulated evergreen groves that flanked the boulevard," noted one source. (Captured Enemy Records, USNA, College Parks, MD.)

B

Color Gallery

A modern African ruler's Mercedes car with regalia. In 1973, a German social worker born in 1905 recalled seeing Hitler in one of his cars: "He drove past. They were having maneuvers, here in the vicinity. One can't say that he looked awful, or anything like that. He drove past and greeted the people. I'm sure it took no great effort for him to drive to the nearby maneuvers." (LC.)

The *Führer* and his Mercedes. A German assistant professor born in 1920 recalled 53 years later of Hitler, "He was standing up, of course, and looked very serious...I stood on the sidewalk, and he drove past in the gutter, which wasn't particularly wide, but all the hullabaloo beforehand was actually much more exciting than the actual event. I already knew beforehand that he had blue eyes." (Walter Frentz.)

Two versions of the same car, a Mercedes-Benz 770K Grosser, as it appeared with bullet-proof glass windows in place at the former Imperial Palace Auto Collection at Las Vegas, NV, courtesy of director Richie Clyne. Note the *Führerstandarte* on the right front mudguard and Hitler's Party brown cap under glass at right. After World War II began with the invasion of Poland on September 1, 1939, he wore a gray-green jacket and black trousers for the duration, a uniform reportedly designed by his young SS adjutants. Also rolled up here is the rear protective shield that served to guard against the type of shots that killed American President John F. Kennedy at Dallas, TX, on November 22, 1963. At the lower left rear wheel in the first shot, the plate glass section shown had a small sign with it that read, "Original, bullet-proof glass fired on by the British Army, and replaced during restoration." (Allen Photographics, Las Vegas, NV.)

A Nazi-era Daimler company poster showing a parked 770K Grosser outside Göring's Berlin Aviation Ministry, which still stands today—minus the Nazi eagle—and was used as a backdrop for the 2009 Tom Cruise movie *Valkyrie*. In 1973, a German comptroller born in 1929 recalled how he had seen his *Führer* in one of the magnificent cars: "I went with my grandma to Stüttgart in May 1937. She lifted me up and they drove on through." (DBM.)

Hitler and his wartime entourage make their exit from one of his favorite Münich restaurants, the *Osteria Bavaria*, now the *Osteria Italiana*. Here, RSD men clear the way for Hitler, who gives a casual, backhanded Nazi salute, followed by his Air Force adjutant, *Luftwaffe* Col. Nikolaus von Below (center). At far right, Hitler valet Heinz Linge of the SS holds open the car door for his *Führer*. (Walter Frentz.)

On the road in a rugged mountain pass. Note the large trunk compartment. (Walter Frentz.)

The *Führer's* 770K limo—with top up—prepares to set off on a motor trip from The Berghof. Note the backup RSD security cars. (Walter Frentz.)

One of the many 770K Grossers in the former Imperial Palace Auto Collection. (Richie Clyne.)

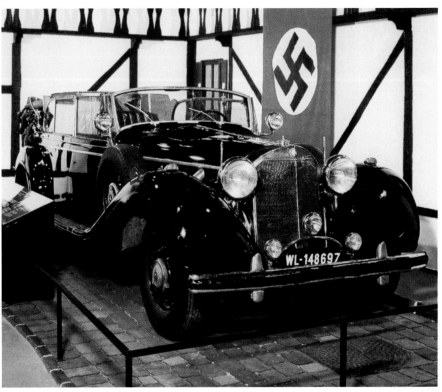

A Hitler Grosser in captivity as it appears now, *Luftwaffe* license plate 148697. (Author's Collection.)

The author with one of Hitler's 770K Grossers at the Nevada State Penitentiary outside Las Vegas, where it was being worked on by the inmates in a work-exchange program with the then Imperial Palace Auto Collection in 2000. (Photo by Dave Hoshaw.)

This is the car that is in the Canadian War Museum at Ottowa, Ontario, Canada, a Type 770 W 150 open tourer, "Liberated from a Salzburg railway siding by the US Army in 1945 in Austria," stated the official Museum guidebook. The car weighs 9,039 pounds, and is capable of a top speed of 106 mph (170 km/h). Stated the brochure on the car at the Museum, "In 1970, the Canadian War Museum bought a historical armored Mercedes-Benz. The 101st US Airborne Division confiscated the car at the end of the war in Europe. The automobile was built in 1940, and bears the serial number 429334 on the still existing plate. This has been confirmed by the order number 366986 in the Daimler-Benz Archives. On July 8, 1940, two days after Hitler triumphantly entered Berlin from the French campaign, the stately Mercedes was driven to Berlin under its own steam and handed over to the Führer's aide-de-camp at the Reich Chancellery's car pool. A few days later, on July 19th, Hitler used this vehicle several times in the course of the next three years. Towards the end of April 1945, the 20th US Tank Division under Maj. Gen. Orlando Ward took part in the fighting towards Salzburg. The division fought near Münich, and marched towards Salzburg. It was on May 4th or 5th when Joe Azara—a lance corporal from the ordnance unit—discovered a heavy car fastened down to an open goods (railroad) wagon on the sidetrack near Laufen, north of Salzburg. He came under fire as he tried to approach, but succeeded in driving the riflemen away, and with the help of some fellow soldiers, got the car on the road, found it drivable, and set off. Shortly afterwards, however, the car came to a stop due to engine damage. The oil in the engine was too light, causing the engine to overheat. The connecting rod was also broken. LCL Azara, however, was up to the task. American newspapers reported that he 'acquired' an engine from the same model car constructed in 1944, which belonged to the 101st Airborne Division. In May 1945, the 20th Armored Division's magazine reported the car was to be transported to Berchtesgaden. The 20th Armored Division left Europe in late July 1945 and arrived at New York harbor on Aug. 6th. Two days later, the Mercedes was unloaded at Castle Island Harbor from the ship *George Shiras*. The same day, the Boston *Globe* printed an illustrated article with the misleading headling, 'Göring's Mercedes is Bullet-Proof.' The article told the Göring legend, which accompanied the car for the next 35 years, as it criss-crossed America and Canada. It was only in 1982—when Ludwig Kösche published his research in the journal *After the Battle # 35*—that the story was refuted. The car was used not by Göring, but by Hitler himself, almost without interruption until 1943. The Mercedes was exhibited all over America, and later stored during 1947-56. It was then auctioned to a car dealer from Toronto, who sold it to collector H.J. O'Connell. After sensitive restoration, the automobile was sold to Claude Pratte, who placed it at the disposal of the Canadian War Museum. The Mercedes has been on exhibit there since 1971." (Photo courtesy the Canadian War Museum, Ottawa, Ontario, Canada.)

Hitler's Grosser arrives at the 1936 Winter Olympic Games at Garmisch-Partenkirchen, Germany, in license plate IIA-22006, a Münich registered vehicle. (HHA.)

A painting of the Marshal Mannerheim Grosser Mercedes as published on the cover of the March 11, 1973, Baltimore *Sunday Sun Magazine* Special Supplement entitled *Wheels*, wherein the car was mistakenly identified by writer Frederic Kelly as one of the *Führer's* own parade vehicles; thus, the *Führerstandarte* on the right front mud guard and the swastika banner draped over the back seat. Note, too, that the rear protective shield has been cranked up. (Painting from the Author's Collection.)

The Battalion Banner/*Standarte* of the 1st SS Regiment Julius Schreck, named for Hitler's famous chauffeur of the *Kampfzeit*/Time of Struggle years of 1919-33, before the *Führer* was named Reich Chancellor on January 30, 1933. (Courtesy George Peterson, National Capital Historic Sales, Springfield, VA, USA.)

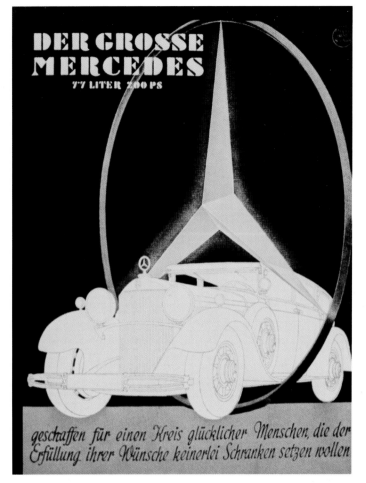

A Daimler company poster advertising the 7.7-liter Great or Grand Mercedes of the 1930s. (Roger Wychgram Collection, Aberdeen, MD.)

The world famous logo complement today. (Blaine Taylor photo.)

A color painting by Mercedes artist Ken Dallison depicting Finnish Marshal Mannerheim standing with his baton in the Grosser Mercedes given him by Hitler on his 75th birthday in 1942. Here, Finnish Army soldiers salute the Marshal, which he returns with his baton. His chauffeur is Kauko Ranta. Note the Finnish flags on the car, and the emplaced bulletproof windows. (DBM.)

From left to right, Hitler's First World War sergeant and Nazi era Eher Verlag publisher Max Amann (1891-1957), Inge Ley, and Dr. Robert Ley (1890-1945), head of the DAF, the German Labor Front. Amann was a *Reichsleiter*/National Leader who served in Hitler's own 16th Bavarian List Reserve Regiment, in which he was awarded the Iron Cross, as was Hitler. Under Amann's keen business management, *Mein Kampf* outsold every book in Germany except the Bible. In 1931, Amann lost his left arm (as seen here) in a hunting accident with a firearm with *Ritter*/Knight von Epp. Dr. Ley divorced his first wife and married soprano singer Inge Spilker Ley on August 20, 1938, and the couple had three children together. He loved her, but also treated Inge cruelly, one day tearing off her clothing so that their guests could admire her body. She fell victim to her husband's alcoholism and brain disease, and shot herself on December 29, 1942. Another account says that she jumped out a window in 1943 over the way that he abused her. A sexual deviant, Dr. Ley hanged himself on the toilet seat of his Nürnberg Prison cell with a towel before he could be tried for war crimes. (Courtesy George Peterson, National Capital Historic Sales, Springfield, VA.)

The 1935 Kaiser Wilhelm II Mercedes-Benz 770K Grand Mercedes Pullman Saloon car, which served as His Majesty's hearse on June 4, 1941. (DBM.)

1930s company views of two open tourers, tops down. (Roger Wychgram Collection, Aberdeen, MD.)

Grosser Pullman Saloon car. (DBM.)

An early use of Mercedes-Benz cars by Hitler occurred at the August 1929 Nazi Party Congress at Nürnberg on what would later be renamed Adolf Hitler Plaza. Standing beneath his outstretched arm are, from left to right, Gauleiter of Nürnberg and Franconia Julius Streicher, Party publisher Max Amann, unknown man, and SA leader Capt. Franz von Pfeffer und Salomon. The windshield is down. Note, too, the arrow directional signal at far right. (HHA.)

Sieg Heil!/Hail Victory! Hitler salutes at the September 1938 parade on Adolf Hitler Plaza, with SS bodyguard Karl Wilhelm Krause standing behind him at left and Viktor Lütze at left of him. Krause was nicknamed Hitler's *Schatten*/Hitler's Shadow. (Photo by Hugo Jaeger.)

The same scene from another angle. Under Hitler's arm are SA Chief of Staff Viktor Lütze (left) and Hess (right). Note the SA unit pennant standard at right (Photo by Hugo Jaeger.)

Command Flags of the Order Police

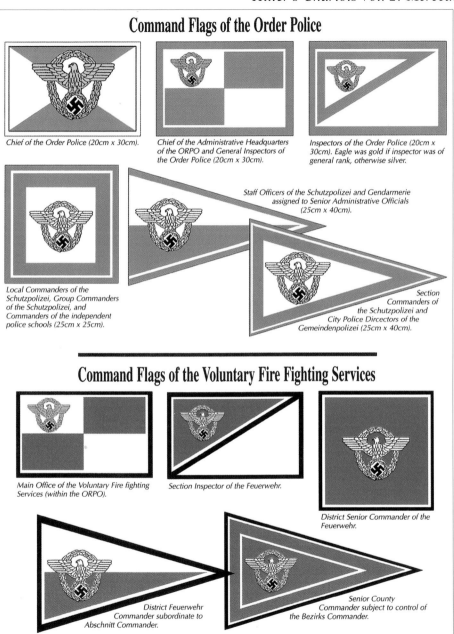

Chief of the Order Police (20cm x 30cm).

Chief of the Administrative Headquarters of the ORPO and General Inspectors of the Order Police (20cm x 30cm).

Inspectors of the Order Police (20cm x 30cm). Eagle was gold if inspector was of general rank, otherwise silver.

Local Commanders of the Schutzpolizei, Group Commanders of the Schutzpolizei, and Commanders of the independent police schools (25cm x 25cm).

Staff Officers of the Schutzpolizei and Gendarmerie assigned to Senior Administrative Officials (25cm x 40cm).

Section Commanders of the Schutzpolizei and City Police Dircectors of the Gemeindenpolizei (25cm x 40cm).

Command Flags of the Voluntary Fire Fighting Services

Main Office of the Voluntary Fire fighting Services (within the ORPO).

Section Inspector of the Feuerwehr.

District Senior Commander of the Feuerwehr.

District Feuerwehr Commander subordinate to Abschnitt Commander.

Senior County Commander subject to control of the Bezirks Commander.

Various command flag car pennants from *The Military Advisor*. (Roger Bender.)

Saluting civilians on the sidewalks of Adolf Hitler Plaza, Nürnberg. (Walter Frentz.)

The same scene from another angle, license plate IA-148768; Hess and Lütze stand at the right front of the car, with the color guards behind the car with the 1923 Blood Flag. (Walter Frentz.)

The view of the marching SA columns as they approached Hitler's car on Adolf Hitler Plaza, which can be seen in the very center of the picture. (Hugo Jaeger.)

Mercedes logo. (DBM.)

The view from behind Hitler's car reviewing stand on Adolf Hitler Plaza, September 1938. Seen here from left to right are Pfeffer, Göring, Krause, Hitler, and Hess as they await the arrival of the endless parading Nazi columns. The 1939 Congress was to be called "The Party Day of Peace," but was cancelled because of Hitler's plan to invade Poland that September. (Walter Frentz.)

German Army troops await the arrival of Hitler's motorcade in Austria, March 13, 1938. (Walter Frentz.)

The *Führer's* motorcade in Linz, Austria, on March 13, 1938; a good rear view showing the various RSD and SS security follow-up cars to his at center right, where he can be seen standing up, saluting. (Walter Frentz.)

Above and Opposite: Hitler's motorcade arriving in Vienna at 5:30 PM on March 14, 1938, followed by three security cars, in turn followed by cars of other dignitaries. Hitler can be seen standing in his own car at center. In opposite photo, note the Austiran Army Troops. (Walter Frentz.)

Cars of the various delegations to the Münich Pact Conference of September 29-30, 1938, in front of the famous war memorial, the Field Lord's Hall. Note license plate #IIB-170125. (Hugo Jaeger.)

RAD men (right) parade past Hitler's 770K. (Frentz)

Hitler gives a Nazi salute at the opening of the House of German Art in Münich, with Kempka at the wheel of the 770K. (Hugo Jaeger.)

The arrival of French Premier Edouard Daladier (left) for the Münich Conference at the municipal airfield on September 29, 1938. Greeting him is German Foreign Minister Joachim von Ribbentrop (right rear). French Ambassador to Germany André Francois-Poncet is the man in the hat at far left, back to camera. (Hugo Jaeger.)

The arrival of British Prime Minister Neville Chamberlain for the Münich Conference at the municipal airfield on September 29, 1938. (Hugo Jaeger.)

Not a Grosser. RFSS Heinrich Himmler (right, center) in his parade car for the Nazi entry into Graz, Austria, March 1938. In the rear seat—looking grim—sits his bodyguard/chauffeur, SS man Josef Kiermaier. (Walter Frentz.)

Ukrainian children stand alongside RFSS Heinrich Himmler's car, license plate SS-1, August 1941. (Walter Frentz.)

Note: Digital photography by Marc Verstraete v.d. Weyer.

M3/68-L.Heck & Sohn, Munich

This "SS-Abschnitt Flandern" car flag was used by SS-Gruppenführer Richard Jungclaus.

Below: In 1937 Abschnitt "XXI" was locatd at Hirschberg in the Riesengebirge (Silezian Mountains) in the Oberabschnitt Südost.

M3/81-E.u.E. Heene, Vienna.

SS car pennants and standards from *The Military Advisor,* Spring 2004 edition. (Roger Bender.)

General SS car pennant and flag from *The Military Advisor,* Spring 2004 issue. (Roger Bender.)

King Boris III of Bulgaria in a formal portrait at *Führer* Headquarters at Ft. Wolf, Rastenburg, East Prussia. He wears the German First World War *Pour le Mérite* (For Your Merit) medal at the throat. (Walter Frentz.)

Rumanian Head of Government and Marshal Ion Antonescu raises his ornate baton aloft in Bucharest during the war. Note that he wears the German *Luftwaffe* Pilot/Observer's Badge on his upper left breast pocket. Note, too, the crossed baton shoulder boards. (LC.)

Not a Grosser. Other Rulers and Mercedes: Britain's Queen Elizabeth II (left) standing next to then West German Chancellor Kurt Georg Kiesinger, a former member of the Nazi Party, during her State Visit to Germany to commemorate the 20th anniversary of the end of World War II in 1965. The limousine is a Mercedes 600 Landaulet model, of which only 59 were built in the 16 years after 1964. Note the West German flag pennant on the left front wing and the British Union Jack hanging from the pole at right—most likely saved from Prime Minister Neville Chamberlain's visit to München in 1938! (Painting by Mercedes artist Ken Dallison, DBM.)

The author (right) as Congressional Press Secretary on Capitol Hill in Wash., DC, to then Rep. Helen Delich Bentley (R, 2nd, MD) in front of her office door with Bulgarian King Simeon II, then an insurance agent living in exile in Madrid, in 1991. He'd left Sofia after the war when Bulgarian Communists drove his family from the throne. A very pleasant man, the exiled monarch spoke fluent English, was married, and had children. After this picture was taken, His Majesty was elected President of Bulgaria, returning home in triumph. He was in Washington to see Mrs. Bentley. The author had written an article on the death of his father, King Boris, that His Majesty had read in Spain. (Previously unpublished, Author's Collection.)

Headquarters Symbols

	Army High Command		
	Army Group		Division
	Army		Brigade
	Group		Regiment
	Corps		Battalion or Detachment

Unit Size

	Army Group		Brigade
	Army		Regiment
	Corps		Battalion or Detachment
	Division		Company

Type of Unit

	Infantry		Motorized Infantry
	Cavalry or Reconnaissance		Artillery
	Armor		Airborne
	Armored Infantry		Mountain

Field Fortifications ΛΛΛΛΛΛΛΛΛΛ

Prepared Defenses ⊓⊔⊓⊔⊓⊔⊓⊔

German Armed Forces map symbols used as car standards. (Courtesy Time-Life Books.)

Examples

NORTH	Army Group North
TENTH	Tenth Army
XVI	XVI Corps
XI	XI Armored Corps
30	30th Infantry Division
2 SS	2d SS Division Das Reich
RAMCKE	Parachute Brigade Ramcke
20	20th Panzer Regiment
91	91st Panzer Grenadier Regiment
2	2d Infantry Regiment
19	19th Artillery Regiment
1 12	1st Battalion, 12th Artillery Regiment
604	604th Antitank Detachment
8MG.	8th Machine-Gun Battalion (Motorized)
2 20	2d Company, 1st Battalion, 20th Infantry Regiment

Bibliography

Adolf Hitler: The dictator and his automobiles article by Blaine Taylor **Centennial Celebration of the Car** by *Automotive News magazine*, 1985

Apex of Glory: Benz, Daimler & Mercedes-Benz 1885-1955 by Blaine Taylor, Church Stretton, UK: Ulric Publishing, 2006

Car edited by John Farndon, New York: Dorling Kindersley, Ltd., 2007

Did You Ever see Hitler? by Walter Kempowski, New York: Equinox Books, 1973

The Hidden Hitler by Lothar Machtan, Cambridge, MA; Basic Books, 2001

Hitler by Dr. Otto Dietrich, Chicago: Henry Regnery Company, 1955

Hitler and the Power of Aesthetics by Frederic Spotts, Woodstock, NY: The Overlook Press, 2003

Hitler's Cars: Transportation for a Dictator article by Edward Morehouse, December 1984 edition of *Car Collector and Car Classic Magazine* on the 770K *Paradewagen*/Car.

Hitler's Headquarters from Beer Hall to Bunker, 1920-45 by Blaine Taylor, Washington, DC: Potomac Books, Inc., 2007

Infiltration: How Heinrich Himmler Schemed to Build an SS Industrial Empire by Albert Speer, New York: Macmillan Publishing Co., Inc., 1981

Inside the Third Reich: Memoirs by Albert Speer, New York: Macmillan Publishing Co., 1970

Karl Brandt: The Nazi Doctor/Medicine and Power in the Third Reich by Ulf Schmidt, London: Hambledon Continuum, 2007

Mercedes-Benz 8: The Supercharged 8-Cylinder Cars of the 1930s, Volumes 1 & 2 by Jan Melin and Sven Hernstrom, Gothenburg, Sweden: Nordbook International

Mercedes-Benz Parade and Staff Cars of the Third Reich: An Illustrated History by Blaine Taylor, Conshohocken, PA: Combined Publishing, Inc., 1999

"A surge of enthusiasm in the city of the 'Foreign Germans' according to Prof. Heinrich Hoffmann's original photo caption. (HHA, U.S. National Archives, College Park, MD.)

The Nüremberg Party Rallies, 1923-39 by Hamilton T. Burden, New York: Frederick A. Praeger, 1967

Parades of the Wehrmacht: Berlin 1934-40 by Horst Scheibert, Atglen, PA: Schiffer Military History, 1997

Spandau: The Secret Diaries by Albert Speer, New York: Macmillan Publishing Co., Inc., 1976

The 12-Year Reich: A Social History of Nazi Germany, 1933-45 by Richard Grunberger, New York: Holt, Rinehart and Winston, 1971

War and Economy in the Third Reich by R.J. Overy, Oxford: Clarendon Press, 1994

We at Porsche: The Autobiography of Dr. Ing. h.c. Ferry Porsche with John Bentley, Garden City, NJ: Doubleday & Co., 1976

The last word, left to right: Hess, unknown SA, Lütze, Krause, Hitler, unknown SS, and Grunminger (covered) with Blood Flag, September 1938, Nürnberg. (Hugo Jaeger.)

Other Books by Blaine Taylor

Guarding the Führer: Sepp Dietrich, Johann Rattenhuber, and the Protection of Adolf Hitler (1993)

Fascist Eagle: Italy's Air Marshal Italo Balbo (1996)

Mercedes-Benz Parade and Staff Cars of the Third Reich (1999)

Volkswagen Military Vehicles of the Third Reich (2004)

Apex of Glory: Benz, Daimler and Mercedes-Benz 1885-1955, Ulric Publishing (2006)

Hitler's Headquarters from Beer Hall to Bunker, 1920-1945 (2007)

Hitler's Chariots. Vol 1., Mercedes-Benz G-4 Cross-Country Touring Car (2009)

Hitler's Engineers: Fritz Todt and Albert Speer/Master Builders of the Third Reich (2010)

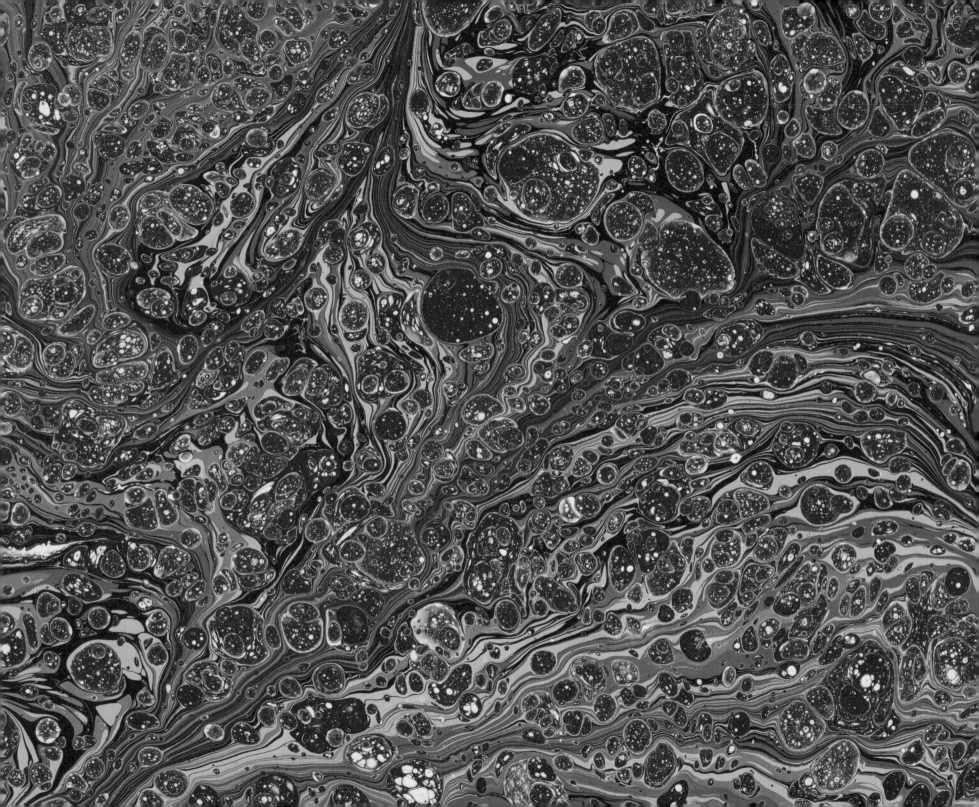